CONCILIUM

Religion in the Eighties

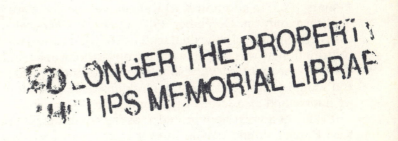

In Memoriam
Karl Rahner

Karl Rahner died in Innsbruck on 30 March this year, nearly a month after his eightieth birthday. Among the innumerable people all over the world who lament the death of this great theologian are not least the sponsors, contributors and friends of *Concilium*. Karl Rahner was one of the founding fathers of our periodical, and he always remained loyal to our main concerns. He had already promised us an article on 'The doctrinal authority of the faithful in the Church' for the number on dogmatic theology planned for 1985.

We cannot here provide a full appreciation of Karl Rahner's outstanding life's work. Obviously he belonged to that small group of theologians who gave the recent Vatican Council its most decisive theological impetus. Our periodical, which does not bear the name *Concilium* by accident, aimed from the start at developing the various forms of stimulation for theological and pastoral renewal in theology and in the Church which had their origin in this Council. This concern was formulated by Karl Rahner, together with Edward Schillebeeckx, as the periodical's initial programme in the first issue, which appeared in January 1965. In addition Karl Rahner had the last word in the number published only in December 1983 to mark *Concilium*'s approaching twentieth birthday. In the final sentence of what turned out to be the final contribution he was able to write for our periodical he said: 'My opinion is in any case that *Concilium* should continue bravely and joyfully to exist and should continue to pursue its task in season and out of season.' This we understand as a legacy of encouragement.

It is for us a great honour and a lasting commitment that the name of Karl Rahner should remain forever linked with *Concilium*.

THE CONCILIUM FOUNDATION

Translated by Robert Nowell

CONCILIUM

Editorial Directors

Concilium 174 (4/1984): Practical Theology

CONCILIUM

List of Members

Editorial Committee: Practical Theology

Directors:

Virgil Elizondo	San Antonio, Texas	USA
Norbert Greinacher	Tübingen	West Germany

Members:

Segundo Galilea	Santiago	Chile
Alfonso Gregory	Rio de Janeiro	Brazil
Frans Haarsma	Nijmegen	The Netherlands
Adrian Hastings	Harare	Zimbabwe
François Houtart	Louvain-la-Neuve	Belgium
Jan Kerkhofs SJ	Louvain	Belgium
Hubert Lepargneur OP	Sâo Paulo SP	Brazil
Anthony Lobo SS	Washington, DC	USA
Angelo Macchi SJ	Milan	Italy
Józef Majka	Wroclaw	Poland
Alois Müller	Lucerne	Switzerland
Thomas Nyiri	Budapest	Hungary
Emile Pin	Poughkeepsie, NY	USA
Karl Rahner SJ	Innsbruck	Austria
Heinz Schuster	Saarbrücken	West Germany
Francisco Soto	Jalapa, Veracruz	Mexico
Yorick Spiegel	Frankfurt, Main	West Germany
Theodore Steeman OFM	Chestnut Hill, Mass.	USA
Wevitavidanelage Don Sylvester	Colombo	Sri Lanka
Rolf Zerfass	Höchberg	West Germany

THE TRANSMISSION
OF THE FAITH
TO THE NEXT GENERATION

Edited by
Norbert Greinacher
and
Virgil Elizondo

English Language Editor
Marcus Lefébure

T. & T. CLARK LTD
Edinburgh

August 1984
T. & T. Clark Ltd, 36 George Street, Edinburgh EH2 2LQ
ISBN: 0 567 30054 4

ISSN: 0010-5236

Typeset by C. R. Barber & Partners (Highlands) Ltd, Fort William
Printed in Scotland by Blackwood, Pillans & Wilson Ltd, Edinburgh

Concilium: Published February, April, June, August, October, December.
Subscriptions 1984: USA: US$40.00 (including air mail postage and packing); Canada:
Canadian$50.00 (including air mail postage and packing); UK and rest of the world:
£19.00 (including postage and packing).

CONTENTS

Part IV
Some Particular Cases

Editorial:
Handing on the Faith to the Next Generation

THE SURVIVAL of every social system depends on whether it succeeds in handing on to the next generation the values which determine its identity. In a stable social situation this presented no particular problem. Customs, traditions, social mechanisms and existing institutions all saw to it that there was an unbroken tradition. Passing this tradition on was a matter of course.

Things are different in a society marked by rapid social change. What was hitherto a matter of course is now called in question. Supporting social institutions change or disappear. Earlier customs and traditions are forgotten or consciously rejected. To take one example: in the sphere of sexual behaviour something like a silent revolution of values has taken place in West Germany in the last twenty years, and no doubt in other countries as well.

The problem of how to pass on the Christian faith today has to be seen against this general social background. Handing on the faith was still a more or less unproblematical affair even at the beginning of our own century in many countries, for the existing cultural and social structures had received their impress from the Church to such an extent that it was often impossible to break out of this mould. The transmission of faith was so firmly integrated in the general process of community social and cultural values that it was often not even necessary for the Church to provide separate instruction for children and young people.

But this situation has now changed fundamentally. There are many indications that the problem of handing on the faith has become acute—dramatically so; indeed that what is at stake is now the Church's very survival. For an interruption to the stream of tradition means a deadly peril for the Church, which cannot live without tradition.

In this context, the different essays in this number of *Concilium* make it clear that the situation takes very different forms in different countries. But the principle which Franz von Baader already postulated in the last century is once again confirmed: 'All life is subject to the paradox that whenever things are supposed to remain as they are, they are not permitted to do so.' In other words, the Christian faith too cannot simply be conserved and passed on under lock and key, like some valuable museum piece. Just at the very point when we strive to remain true to this Christian faith, our testimony must be new and different in a new social situation. Anyone who thinks that he can serve the cause of Jesus by constantly repeating the same formulas is actually thereby preventing the communication of what he has at heart.

Another recognition seems to be crystallising out too. More than ever before, handing on the faith is going to be one important function of the local Christian congregation. The congregation is the place where people learn what being a Christian means: this insight is increasingly determining catechetical discussion. And something else is emerging at the same time: passing on faith is not merely a matter of particular verbal formulations or cognitive learning. If faith wants to be something that is truly alive in the coming generation as well, it must be experienced in practice: in everyday actions and behaviour, in the celebration of worship, in experiences that are emotional in kind.

However, one thing is hopeful: the source that provides 'significance' in modern life is also limited (Habermas). People feel the need for the social institution that is able to provide convincing evidence that there is a meaning in human life and in society. It depends on Christians and the Christian churches whether they can testify to the things of Jesus in such a way that men and women experience this faith as offering something that is relevant for their own lives.

NORBERT GREINACHER
VIRGIL ELIZONDO
Translated by Margaret Kohl

PART I

The Problem

André Godin

'Christians by Birth': Psychological Alienation or Liberation in The Spirit?

MANY CHRISTIANS, whether parents or pastors, are surprised or distressed by the resistance which they encounter in baptised young people growing up to adulthood. Their surprise is particularly acute when faced with manifestations of an allergic rejection of a Christianity which, in all good faith, they would wish to be a liberating influence but of which the mere presentation is seen as alienating, even poisonous. In Germany this allergy has found expression in the famous book by Tilman Moser, whose virulence should not mask the relevance of his desire to free himself from 'being poisoned by God ... the vindictive stop-gap for ignorance and the impotence of society'.[1]

In order to measure and understand this enormous gulf between the liberating *intentions* of Christian educators and the anti-alienating *positions* already adopted by their hearers, one may first consider the pedagogical aspect. Might not the catechetical process introduce dissonances between the cognitive content of the Good News being proclaimed and a certain climate of rigidity (authoritarian? boring?) unconsciously created by teachers who are neither liberated themselves nor even free to decide to teach these courses?[2] One may also look, with the possibility of discovering many useful observations, to sociologists or analysts of language as they reveal perceptible discrepancies between certain ways in which ecclesiastical power or its semantics may function and the cultural, literary or scientific evolution of numerous countries around the Mediterranean basin and on both sides of the North Atlantic.[3]

The psychological perspective

The *liberation-alienation* antinomy, as an essential issue in the transmission of Christianity, will be examined in this article in a different perspective, as complementary to the discordances which may be called external, previously mentioned. Fifty years of work published on the psychology of (the Christian) religion allow us better to define and to divide up an area of dissonances, both cognitive and affective, in which the process of transmission of the liberating meanings of the Christian message can easily become bogged down. Their accumulation whilst a baptised child is growing up finally produces an 'alienation', in a sense to be defined, to which he succumbs or from which he frees himself by an act of rejection.

Alienation is defined in the *Lexis* (Larousse) as 'the state of a man who, living in social

3

conditions determined by symbols and institutions, submits himself to them blindly and is thereby distracted from consciousness of his real problems'. From the psychological standpoint, we shall retain the concept of alienation through *the maintenance within the unconscious* of certain fears or desires, a process encouraged by a socially determinant system of symbols. It seems that certain subjects receive the Christian message in a way which prevents them from being born, or reborn into their own true nature as a man or a woman in the real world. The psychological approach consists, then, in discovering *how* religious discourse (Christian, in this instance) speaks to people's desires or fears, how it makes itself understood *in practice* in the conscious and unconscious psyche. Although it is now readily used in sociological studies, the concept of alienation does not, of course, figure in the Biblical lexis with this particular meaning.

Liberation, on the other hand, is well represented in the vocabulary of both Old and New Testaments by words derived from the same root: setting free, to make free, freedom, free. In the Old Testament, these words are antonyms of captivity (in the literal or figurative sense) and frequently employed. In the New Testament, one discovers first of all their central place in Pauline dialectics, in which they designate (25 times) the opposite of slavery: freedom from sin, demons, the law, death. In different periods, places and ideologies, certain additional meanings have become grafted onto them: liberation from diseases, economic or political servitude, injustices, racial or sexual discrimination and, more generally, oppressive relationships based on the master-slave concept. The frequency of these examples (literal or figurative) contrasts with their infrequent use in the Synoptics (6 times) and in St John's Gospel (a single passage in which the word is repeated three times in succession): 'The truth will make you free . . ., "How is it that you say, 'You will be made free'?" . . . So if the son makes you free, you will be free indeed' (John 8:32, 33, 36).

The evidence and reflections presented in this aticle may be related to these Johannine verses. To be born of the Spirit is to attain to the truth of the desire of the Father shown forth by Jesus and, through the same process, to find oneself gradually liberated from the alienation of a religion which originates in the desires of man. It is a fact, as Freud has stressed, that man's desire sustains a religiosity which, psychologically, he uses to confine within his unconscious some part of his real problems: finitude, dependence, conflicts (even in love), death. To be born again of the Spirit is to accept an offer of adoptive sonship in order to conform oneself to it actively and in truth: to discover oneself to be free in symbolic relationships whilst recognising that one is determined by historically-imposed situations. How does this process become aborted and result in alienation?

1. AN INITIAL ALIENATION (INCULTURATION)

Every religion, and also lack of religion, impinges on a child as soon as he becomes aware of language and thus communicates with people who preside over his entry into a culture. This entry is effected under the *successive dominance* of the family, the school, the media and social milieux which are first of all *imposed* on the child. A little later, during adolescence, groups or milieux which are *chosen* make their appearance: leisure activities, friendships, groupings which are joined freely; later still, professional, artistic, ideological, sporting and other associations.

This introduction into a culture, the starting point for human growth, constitutes an 'alienation', if one insists on this word, in the definition recalled earlier. The agents of inculturation condition and, to a certain extent, structure the child's affectivity in non-chosen relationships (the family network), impose behaviour patterns and habits, mould anarchic impulses to a social order, restrain desires by delaying their fulfilment or repress them in the unconscious by charging them with guilt. This moulding into shape, which is indispensable for social life, takes place with the aid of many *words which are alien* to the cries (appeals, furious outbursts, protests, tears) of desire itself. The totality of the automatic reflexes internalised in this way is usually termed the *super-ego*.

Marked by this 'colonisation' which conditioned its entry into the adult world, the *ego* may gradually become free, but never starting from scratch nor in a state of individual isolation. Firstly, it constructs for itself an imaginary space, desert or promised land, a refuge rich in resources, at first in the service of a fantasy of omnipotence (*ideal-self*, according to certain authors), later enriched by various models with which it partially identifies (*ideal of the self*) which diversify and, particularly, soften the rigidity of the super-ego, without necessarily opening up the ego to the other as a potential subject of friendship and love. The amorous encounter, on the basis of demands which are sexual in origin, constitutes, for a man or a woman in most of the cultures under consideration, one of the decisive tests of maturity: will the inevitable divergence of desires survive in faithfulness and love? Or will it become the cause of incessant conflicts in which each partner becomes exhausted in an egocentric struggle for domination? A struggle in which forgiveness itself may be booby-trapped . . .

How do Christian symbols come to be associated with these various drives and these different stages of growth? Drawing on research carried out in recent years (omitting here references which may easily be found elsewhere[4]), this article will suggest how alienating associations come to be attached to certain basic *words* of the religious and Christian lexis: *God* and *his attributes, sin, Jesus crucified, love*. Of course, psychology will allow the 'receivers' of the Christian message, and occasionally its 'transmitters' (parents, speech, school textbooks, preaching), to speak for themselves. It goes without saying that the latter may themselves already be victims of alienation.

2. AFFECTIVE OR COGNITIVE DISSONANCES

How does a religion (Christianity) make itself understood, first by the child, then as he grows up? *In fragments*, assimilated on the basis of the human and religious desires of the growing children.

(a) God: early childhood within the family

The most prestigious word which the child receives in his lexical heritage. A category which is devoid of meaning in itself, the idea of God designates and creates a psychological space beyond the world, people and societies. God is a *space* opened up to desire within semantic reality. Therefore, one may hear this:

(i) God: ally of the ego

Charles (aged 6) is unjustly punished. He is told off for what he has not done, or has not done on purpose. He appeals against his father and mother, shouting: 'I tell you: *God knows* I didn't do it!' Jacqueline (aged 7) feels unwanted in a family in which the boys seem to her to be favoured. In bed, she repeats ten or twenty times over: 'Nobody loves me any more. But you, God, *you love me*'—and finally falls asleep.

An omniscient witness to whom one can appeal (Charles), a presence renewing the certainty of being loved (Jacqueline). In Christian terms, God has perhaps not spoken his final word. Nevertheless: the Word has functioned in the service of the ego. Just judge or friend of the heart, the imaginary space takes on a supplementary life, with the drives directed towards growing up, dignity, unconditional love.

(ii) God: cause of anxiety

Gretchen (aged 4): 'Can God really *see everything*? Through the door, through the walls?' Having discussed the matter with her brother (aged 6) who reaffirms what he has learned from adults, she concludes: 'Anyway, I think God can see *best* through *glass*'.

Peter (aged 6): 'Daddy, is it true what the neighbour says? That the lightning struck the tower of Christus Kirche because they're Protestants?' After his father's reply (not quoted) he remains thoughtful, then objects: 'All the same, God is *the Protestants' God as well*'.

Omniscience ('seeing everything') which seems disturbing for personal privacy (Gretchen), power ('divine lightning') deliberately hostile to the Protestants (Peter): these children preserve an attitude of compromise and questioning. God is badly understood: they become defensive. A conflict, without surrender.

(iii) God: centre of the super-ego

Marco (aged 4) fidgets on his chair, then falls. Mummy declares: 'I told you to sit still. You see: *the Good Lord has punished you*!' Marco lowers his eyes and remains crestfallen.

Lucia (aged 6) is put in charge of her 4-year-old brother. When her mother comes back: what a sight! 'Aren't you ashamed? You took advantage of my absence to do that! And God, did you even think of *God*? Who is always there . . . *How shameful*!' Lucia goes red, her hands are shaking when she puts them in her mouth. Finally, she vomits.

These children no longer say anything. Ten or twenty times a month they hear God, that word, associated with reproaches, constraints, reasons for being ashamed (whatever these may be). The mechanism of the super-ego, an important component of the awakening of the socio-moral sense, has become taken over by God, made sacred and absolute. Desires for life, movement, curiosity, dirtiness, are charged with guilt, then repressed, even *as desires*, associated with the anguish of transgression. The desire-word is banished (it may remain so in the scrupulous obsessive). All that can be done is to go red, tremble, vomit. The body exhibits the stigmata of the alienation of desire. The super-ego is not an illness. But childish affectivity contracts an illness when the super-ego is haunted by the perverse God.[5] Desiring is a sin.

(b) Almighty Father: children undergoing religious instruction

The philosophical attributes of divine transcendence attain their maximum degree of acceptance between the ages of 8 and 10[6] (greatness, omniscience, omnipotence, activeness). They will invade the psychology of children attending catechism classes even if their teachers speak to them in rather different tones from the lexical range normally found in most families: Father, Son and Spirit (removing the ambiguity of the word God), a welcoming and joyful atmosphere, prayers of adoration. 'Religious instruction classes aren't boring', declared the great majority of children (aged 6–12) in France in 1975, even if 60% still stated that they were bored at mass. The fascination of an interventionist Omnipotence (modifying the causalities and chances of the world) is, however, at a high level here and finds fuel for the imagination in Bible stories (especially from the Old Testament) well translated into pictures or cartoon. Is not the desire for omnipotence at the centre of the Ideal-self, at the origin of a magical way of thinking which man will never abandon completely? Is not the 'almighty' Father useful when some harsh reality drives men to address petitions for favours to him?[7]

Omnipotence: cognitive discordance

(i) Can God make you do what you really do not want to do?

Correct answer: NO. 7-year-olds: 11%; 9-year-olds: 35%; 11-year-olds: 82%; 13-year-olds: 95%. Correct answers are always less frequent among girls than boys in research carried out before 1970. The fact that at the age of nine two children out of three believe that God can possibly violate their liberty reveals a cognitive discordance. Catechism classes would tend rather to teach the opposite. But the desire, which is typically religious (in the general sense of that word), is probably sustained by Bible pictures and stories. Now, if discordance is to be avoided, a choice must be made sooner or later: the Omnipotence invoked by desire does not coincide with that of the Father who does not send legions of angels even for the sake of the well-loved son, the prophet in Jerusalem of a particular kind of love which excludes violent intervention.

'Mummy, if God is good and almighty, as people say, why didn't he stop the flood sweeping away Elisabeth and her parents although we'd all prayed together at school to be protected?' (Mary, aged 8). If he is the Master of the waters (responsible for a Great Flood designed to punish people, but also of the end of the Flood), why did he not prevent the flood itself?

'But *wasn't Yahweh the God of the Egyptians as well?*' That question, asked after the miracle story of the crossing of the Red Sea (by John, an English Protestant, exceptionally precocious for his 10 years) proved to be insoluble for three-quarters of the English children under 14 who were questioned. Identification with the power of Yahweh is so captivating for the imagination that it represses, cognitively, the Christian positing of new desires such as those shown forth by Jesus the prophet.

Praying to obtain benefits

'My will be done!' This would be the cry of the young infant if he could speak. 'My will be done by obtaining it from the interventionist Omnipotence!', would be the petition of innumerable believers (of all religions). These prayers for benefits, defensible as expressions of desires, prolong a discordance which results, for many, in the abandonment of any petition. Whatever may be the case with regard to this possible eclipse of the prayer of petition, the opinion according to which a particular *modification* of the conditioning factors, the interactions or the hazards of daily life may be causally obtained by prayers, deliberately directed towards obtaining these 'favours', is widely held (at least 50%) at 13 but it gradually diminishes with age in all the samples of various Christian denominations in five countries and rarely exceeds 15% at the age of 20. Does not this evolution, culturally evident as a fact (in no way ruling out the Christian prayer of petition), raise questions about catechetical education? Being Christian, it can surely not base daily prayer '*in order to* obtain' benefits on the constant possibility of miracles, even small ones, of that type.

Moreover, a religion which, through prayer, frequently obtained[8] such modifications to accommodate desires thwarted by reality, would result psychologically in the worst kind of dependence: every obstacle which revealed human finitude, faced with the harsh realities (hostile or even cruel happenings, injustices, diseases, imminent death) would then drive men back—an image which is nowadays indefensible—to the goodwill of an omnipotent Prince according his favours to those who beseech him humbly. That religion, inevitably centred upon the magical techniques needed to obtain the fulfilment of desires, would be no more than a resigned idolatry, directed towards an unknown, alienating god, repressing the true nature of our human condition. The cultural evolution just mentioned, moving away from such an image of the divine, would therefore seem rather inclined to give a hearing to the concept of an alliance which would symbolically renew the whole system of relationships between God and man: 'I call you servants no longer, but friends' (John 15:15) because I have made *known* to you completely the *desires* of the Father. The cognitive discordance, threatening alienation, is removed by this parting word. Liberating, as an offer of love, this word soon condemned the one who pronounced it to breathe his last. But, as every Christian knows, since the first Pentecost a second Breath has unceasingly made his followers better understand and express what had been said and lived out by the one whose name was 'exalted above every name' by the Father. From the Christian standpoint, the Omnipotence of the Father is now present in this offer: the gift of a Spirit who makes men and women speak and act, in accordance with his own desires, henceforth grafted onto theirs. This profound mutation of the love-relationship (agapè) gives a place of honour to the most wretched outcasts of mankind.

(c) Jesus as a model: the crucified

Agnès (aged 6): 'Mummy, didn't *the good thief* cry a little bit anyway, because the cross was hurting him?' Imprudently guided by her mother towards an identification which was beyond her powers ('If you feel a little pain during the operation, remember that good Lord Jesus didn't cry on the cross'), Agnès spontaneously found herself a model to identify with which was more accessible to her *ideal of the self*, under too much pressure from her mother's imagination. This new compromise reaction in a young child raises, however, the problem of an alienation hidden in certain devotional teachings based on identifications which are . . . suggested. A century or two of dolorist literature (even excluding books of Christian devotion) have no doubt emphasised the crucifixion as a privileged moment in the life of Jesus considered as a model. In any case, this theme has recurred over twenty centuries of Christianity. What should be internalised in a partial identification: the situation, imaginatively re-created, of the crucified one?—or the meaning, lovingly contemplated, of the desires, the words and the actions of Jesus which brought about his trial, condemnation and death? It is not for psychology to answer this question, which is, however, 'crucial': the first option directs devotion towards an *idealisation* of the suffering hero; the second bases devotion on an *identification* through the partial internalisation of desires directed towards the outcasts of today, according to the Spirit of the Lord.

(d) God: Love

A certain kind of teaching and a certain type of spirituality strongly accentuate affective language to proclaim the Good News: God *is* Love, Tenderness, Forgiveness and even . . . Risk (obviously an attractive one) of encountering that Other. In comparison with a dry memorisation of doctrine, which predominated in the past, today's emphasis restores an essential dimension: the *enjoyment* of desire entering into a relationship of love *received*. A dimension which is essential, but not all-sufficient. Even in human love, the amorous encounter involves the mutual discovery of the divergence of desires. *Erôs* is marked by this divergence in the body in its radical—sexual—differentness. The infiltration of the dominance-submission relationship, quite out of place here, is in several of our cultures the danger which threatens the loving union in its enjoyment and in its faithfulness in partially internalising certain desires of the other partner during the waning of the history of the couple. Can a similar danger threaten the agapè? Yes, if the element of pathos in the Christian experience begins, through an unbelievable impoverishment, to make play with capital letters (Love, Tenderness, Forgiveness) to obscure the *desire-words* which, in the first-born Son, expressed the specific nature of that agapè: identification, deliberately sought, with those who have the greatest need to be set free in their human reality. The 'you have done it unto me' is one of those desire-words, specific if not central to the new network of human relationships of which Jesus reveals the plan. It is the task of the exegetes and theologians to seek out and clarify, for our time, other desire-words which are really basic to Christianity. Psychologically, let it suffice that we have pointed out that an Immense Love, whose Supreme Authority takes the initiative and which it is enough for us to receive as a satisfaction of our desires or the fulfilment of our emptiness could spiritually only be accepted without any liberty. An absolute alienation in place of salvation, it would be the transformation of which man spontaneously dreams, rapidly ending in a nightmare of suffocation. The prophet Jesus, living on in each believer through his Spirit, said nothing to justify such a spirituality of suffocation. One must still re-establish, in transmitting his message of love in the name of the Father, the acceptance, to be ceaselessly deepened at the cognitive level, of the movement of identification with the outcasts which inspired his incarnation and offers itself to our freedom as the essential structure of his agapè. 'To abandon oneself so that the gift may become effective' (Pierre Rousselot)—of course, but this is at the same time to be reborn into the newness of the movement and the plan which invite the ego to actively preferential fellowship with the outcasts of men. The progressive experience of contemplative internalisation and active externalisation: Christian perceptions are always marked by compromises in the alliance of desires. On this point, the agapè is no exception.

3. BEING REBORN TO LANGUAGE ACCORDING TO THE SPIRIT

Baptised at birth, at the instigation of his parents' faith, the young premature Christian later receives a religious and Christian language. To be born again, perceiving in that language a liberation in the Spirit, will be neither easier nor more difficult for him than . . . for Nicodemus, or any other adult on hearing a voice speaking to him of love where he had at first only located his own desire.

Less fortunate than Nicodemus, some young Christians heard a language encumbered with dissonances which threatened to draw Christian words into areas where they had nothing to say: the super-ego, the fantasy of omnipotence, idealisation protected from reality.

The earliest layer of this contamination: the parental gods ridiculously used in the service of their educative aims. Developing parental awareness, by directing their attention to the use of 'god', which can be easily pinpointed (see *supra* II.1) and debated, could become an objective of all adult Christians if they are convinced that Good News is not identical with Good Morals, nor with Holy Obedience.

A deposit from schooldays sometimes worsens, unconsciously, the initial family situation. One would wish to find *Yahweh* (and not God) behind pictures of grandiose interventions in conformity with Judaic symbolism. One might also propose 'prayers *in union with* . . .' people in trouble, when 'prayers *for* . . .' the material modification of that trouble are being formulated. A wish and a proposal which will obviously not be put into effect tomorrow. But, on reflection, why not?

The excessive nature of the identifications which are suggested for the ideal of the self, and the affective emphasis directed towards God-Love without a cognitive counterpoint provided by the meaning of the desire-words which mark out the manifestation of agapè according to the Scriptures, will quickly have suggested to the reader other loci of discordances which produce conflict (which are partly repressed), established towards the end of adolescence (which is sometimes retarded) and laboriously unscrambled (at the age of 30 or 40) through some kind of therapy . . . At the same time the author's personal conviction was being affirmed: the liberating axis of Christianity can begin, or begin again to move only by starting from the desire-words which are most specific to it, re-actualised today and then tomorrow in the freedom of perception according to the Spirit.

Translated by L. H. Ginn

Notes

1. T. Moser *Gottesvergiftung* (Frankfurt 1978), which should be read in conjunction with his *Grammatik der Gefühle* (1979). In French, a good critical survey of recent books, denouncing, sometimes to the point of vomiting up, the 'poison which the Church contained in its foundations', has just been produced by J.-F. Six 'Le Christianisme au banc des accusés' *Etudes* 358(4) avril 1983, 535–548.

2. The surveys of the sociologist Giancarlo Milanesi in Umbria, *Religione e liberazione* (Turin, 1971) were quite unambiguous on that subject in the social group studied. Read his final conclusions on a religious education 'encouraging the development of young people, but failing to liberate them' (*op. cit.* pp. 271–282).

3. For some interesting discoveries on semantics in closed auto-production, see F. Dassetto *Analyse du discours religieux et sociologie* (Louvain 1973), *Production liturgique et Judaïsme* (Louvain 1975) and 'La Production homilétique catholique' *Social Compass* 27(4) 1980, 375–396. For a brief synthesis of ideas on the necessary confrontations with a changing culture, read the 'seven challenges to be taken up' by the institutional church of the future, *L'Eglise institutionnelle dans l'avenir* (Pro Mundi Vita, 82) (Brussels July 1980 28 pp.). For a general problematics of sociological alienation, re-read V. Cosmao *Changer le monde* (ch. VI: 'Perversion et renaissance du christianisme') (Paris 1981).

4. According to the period studied, one could refer to e.g. A. Godin *L'Athéisme dans la vie et la culture contemporaines* (vol. I, ch. II.3: 'Croissance psychologique et tentation d'athéisme') (Paris 1967) pp. 269–292; 'Some Developmental Tasks in Christian Education' in *Research on Religious Development* ed. M. Strommen (New York 1971) pp. 109–154, or A. Godin *Psychologie des expériences religieuses* (Paris 1981). (Areas covered: Mediterranean basin, both sides of the North Atlantic, Germany, Sweden).

5. M. Bellet *Le Dieu pervers* (Paris 1979) presents brilliant evocations of the guilt which results, particularly, from this precociously conditioned misunderstanding.

6. For children attending catechism classes in France, the scientific study of J.-P. Deconchy *Structure génétique de l'idée de Dieu* (Brussels 1967) is irreplaceable and ought to be repeated.

7. For the regrettable tendency of the word *providence* to superimpose itself on the word *chance* (of which it hinders the correct usage), two references and a few comments will be found in *Psychologie des expériences religieuses* (1983²) pp. 33–37.

8. This hypothesis is formulated here in order better to reveal the cognitive-affective incoherence between the conscious content of the invocation and the latent idea (on the subject of Omnipotence) which underlies it. The financial commitment and the considerable sacrifices which result from this *fixation* of desire on the *content* of the invocation (the 'favour' solicited) have no direct connection with the expression of confidence which could bring believers (of any religion) to express *all* their desires in prayer. Once the Trinitarian Divinity, with his own desires of love, is better known, it may even be thought that this constant confrontation of desires, partially divergent in prayer and its instances of unfulfilment, is essential to Christian prayer. Psychologically speaking, one would therefore be more suspicious of an elitist or idealistic prayer, as being a subtle way of avoiding the shock of the real and the inevitable distance which must be maintained between our own desires and those which the Spirit inspires in us, without any pretentions of realising them other than through a gradual modification of each one of us.

Oscar Beozzo

Catechetical Problems in a Changing Society: Brazil

1. THE CHANGES IN SOCIETY

THE PROBLEMS that affect catechesis in Brazilian society include the demographic, economic, social, political and cultural changes that have taken place, as well as those related to the particular history and structure of the Church in Brazil.

The demographic change has been a three-fold increase in the population between 1940 and 1980, from 41 to 120 million, reaching 129 million in 1983. Half the population is now aged under 19.

In the economic field, the traditional agrarian economy has given way to industry and the countryside has undergone a process of modernisation. Agriculture today counts for scarcely 10% of gross national product. The rural population has been displaced into the cities: in 1940, 70% of the population lived in the country, whereas today the figure is a bare 30%. Some cities have had a literal population explosion: São Paulo had one million inhabitants in 1940 and thirteen million in 1983. Rio de Janeiro and its satellites have nine million.

The labour market has changed profoundly with industrialisation and modernisation: the primary sector accounts for only 29% of those in employment, industry for 25% and services for 46%. The position of women has also changed rapidly. In 1940 women accounted for 15% of the workforce, and 20% in 1970, but by 1980 the number of women in the labour market had doubled, from six to twelve million, reaching 30% of the workforce. In the lowest age group, fifteen and sixteen years old, this figure is as high as 40%. This has been one of capitalism's responses to the recession: in order to keep up profit margins, male employees are dismissed and replaced by women and girls. This distorting effect of the massive increase in the number of girls employed has had a direct result on their wages: in 1970 the average female wage was 60% of the male wage; by 1980 this had dropped to 42% of the average male wage for equal work.

The mass influx of workers from the land to the cities has created a population in continual migration. In 1980, forty million Brazilians were migrant workers, living far from the place where they were born and brought up.

Culturally, the scene is dominated by three simultaneous phenomena: uprooting, the spread of basic education and the diffusion of a mass culture through radio and television. Illiteracy in those aged 15 or over has declined from 50.3% of the population in 1950 to

25% in 1980. University entrances have gone up from 90,000 in 1960 to 1.3 million in 1980. The transistor radio has drawn the peoples of the interior out of their traditional isolation and 1,200 radio and 120 television stations have revolutionised the information network, as well the habits and customs of the people, who have often moved straight from illiteracy to a culture of image and sound.

2. CHANGES IN THE CHURCH

The Church has changed along with society, the basic change being a progressive commitment to social questions, beginning in the 1930s and increasing in strength from the end of the 1950s. The Council came like a hurricane, freeing theology and Church discipline from the straitjacket of time, but also coming into conflict with the faith and religious customs of the masses. Medellín established the position of the Church in the face of the oppression rife on the continent of Latin America, the injustice of the international order and internal colonialism.

Inside Brazil, the age-old shortage of clergy was aggravated by a massive closure of seminaries and by the exodus of a large number of secular priests and religious who left their ministry.

The changes in society and the Church not only brought about a break in the traditional channels of catechesis, the family and the rural communities, but also affected the content of faith and changed the challenges and questions that reflection and practice of faith have to face. On top of this, there is a new problem in the linguistic field. Formerly, there was a certain *impasse* between a faith based on a written culture and a largely illiterate population. Today the Church is still firmly attached to its written culture, whereas the bulk of the population is more and more involved in a culture stemming from the mass media, television in particular.

All these changes have, for the first time, posed not only the problem of how to hand on the faith, but also that of re-socialising adults uprooted by migration and the changes in society, who no longer feel at home in a Church which has changed much of its outlook and introduced innovations in its liturgy and prayer.

3. THE POLITICAL DIMENSION OF FAITH

Added to all this, the catechetical problems of Brazil cannot be divorced from the exceptional political situation which the country has experienced over the past twenty years.

In 1964 a military coup installed a dictatorship which has not yet run its course. These have been twenty years in which the country has been forced into a deeper involvement in Western capitalist economy, with opportunities made and conditions created for the implantation of multinational enterprises, and the economy of the country subordinated to the tough requirements of the international money market. The first phase of this process saw a new impetus given to industrial development, speeded up through a process of holding down wages and increasing profits, at enormous social cost. The second phase, with export markets strangled by recession, landed the country in the worst economic crisis of its history, with the destruction of its productive capacity, deep recession, unemployment and a brutal fall in levels of income.

The Church, which had initially supported the 1964 coup, gradually became disenchanted with the regime, becoming a critical body within society and linking its fortunes more and more with the social classes excluded from the economic benefits of development. During the period of most brutal repression, from 1968–73, when all protest was stifled, the Church spoke out against the tortures and political assassinations that were taking place. The Commissions for Justice and Peace and, later, on the popular level, the Centres for the Defence of Human Rights, played an essential part in the resistance struggle against dictatorship and repression. The Church was an important ally in struggles for political amnesty, for the restitution of the Statute of Rights and of constitutional guarantees for individuals and institutions, for the holding of elections, for the freedom of trade unions and the right to strike. It sheltered many of the teachers persecuted by the government and forced to flee from the State universities in its own universities and study centres. Many political militants found room to carry on their work of organising the people in the Church's activities in the base communities. In the countryside, there was a growing alliance forged between the Church and peasants dispossessed from their land, between the Church and smallholders threatened by absentee landlords and forced-purchase schemes, between the Church and the unions. In the industrial heart of the country, São Paulo and particularly the districts known as ABC (the municipalities of Santo Andre, São Bernardo and São Caetano), the great industrial strikes of 1978–9 and 1980 were strongly supported by the ecclesial base communities, and, when the Union was proscribed and public meetings at places of work forbidden, the bishop opened the gates of the cathedral and the other churches to workers wanting to hold meetings.

This drawing apart of the Church from the State gave it a new position in civil society; by distancing itself from the economic, social and political State project, allied to the multinationals and the bourgeoisie, it drew closer to the popular classes, but also—which gave it a more combative stance—to the intellectuals and the universities. A broad area of cooperation and understanding grew up between large sectors of the working class and the Church. These factors are crucial in the development of the Church's practice, its commitment to the masses, and the establishment of a certain image of the Church, of its message and its practices, which has become the framework for catechesis of the new generations. Today, resistance to the Church and its message stems from the ruling classes in society, shaken by this desertion by an erstwhile ally.

However, to translate this favourable new situation into work of evangelisation and handing on and deepening of faith, requires other elements, such as the reorganising of the context of religious socialisation.

4. ADULT EVANGELISATION AND CATECHESIS IN THE BASE COMMUNITIES

Where people are uprooted, exploited, have to struggle to earn their living and even to survive, catechesis can no longer be simply a matter of one generation handing the faith on to the next.

The whole question of faith is posed in a particularly acute way for the adults of the present generation, men and women who ask themselves the meaning and application of their faith in the extreme situations they are obliged to bear and to face up to. This is why the most significant experiences in the field of deepening and maturing in faith have been found less with children and young people and more among adults engaged in labour and their families, and with responsibilities in the community, unions and politics.

It is true to say that adult catechesis has come to occupy the central place in the activities of the Church in Brazil today. Not adults taken as individuals, but as members of a community involved in debating the needs of the group, and of the wider community, and the challenges and threats hanging over the lives of the poorest. It is in the heart of the base communities that the ways of handing on the faith of the future are being opened up. The bishops of Brazil recognise that: 'in their life practice, they (the base communities) have found surprising ways of achieving an incarnate evangelisation, catechesis and liturgy, all closely linked to the word of God. In their "hunger and thirst for justice" they have found ways of putting ecumenism into practice on the ground. Furthermore, they are developing a process of participative intercommunication and of forming a critical sense in the face of the massification produced by the communications media. In their constant effort in the fields of action, reflection and celebration, they offer an alternative education to those who are looking for a new society, one in which individualism, competition and profit will give way to justice and brotherhood'.[1]

The originality of the course followed by the base communities lies not only in their emphasis on educating Christian adults in their faith, nor in their dimension of collective quest, but rather in their capacity continually to unite faith and life. There is a constant and daily search to read reality in the light of faith, to keep one's eyes open to reality and one's ears attuned to the word of God. 'They run on twin tracks. One is the track of life, of human experience, of our way forward, our history. The other is the track of the message, of the word that expresses the faith of the Church, its tradition and understanding of the word of God. The train of catechesis runs on these parallel tracks'.[2]

In its document on Renewed Catechesis, the Episcopal Conference makes this adult catechesis the model for all catechesis: 'The community catechesis of adults, far from being an appendix or complement, should be the ideal model and reference to which all other forms of catechetical activity should be subordinate'.[3]

In the base communities, the catechetical work par excellence has proved to be the Bible, and the basic theme is the interaction between faith and life, echoing the words of Paul VI in *Evangelii nuntiandi*: 'Evangelisation would not be complete if it did not take account of the unceasing interplay of the Gospel and man's concrete life, both personal and social' (n. 29).

Another aspect that gives a new and vigorous character to the faith experience of the base communities is that they are more and more becoming the way in which the Church is present in the world of the poor. The first result of this has been the discovery that the poor are becoming the evangelisers of the rest of the Church: 'The commitment to the poor and the oppressed and the rise of the base communities has helped the Church to discover the evangelising potential of the poor, inasmuch as these pose a constant challenge to the Church, calling it to conversion, and because many of them put into practice in their lives the evangelical values of solidarity, service, simplicity and openness to receiving God's gift.'[4]

As the people of the poor, growing and organising themselves in the light of the word of God, the base communities have engaged themselves further and further in a practice of social and political involvement which has had profound repercussions on society. This social and political dimension of evangelisation is nothing other than what should be present in all the Church's actions: 'The new dimension the base communities added was the fact of offering the simple poor people an opportunity within the Church of participating in the evangelisation of society through the struggle for justice. In this sense, the base communities have proved themselves to be a special focus of education for justice as an instrument of liberation'.[5]

The experience of the base communities has led the Church in Brazil along new paths, making the episcopal conference itself seek to take account of the wisdom of the people in its pronouncements, to take up the themes relevant to them and to incorporate the analysis, concepts and language of the popular struggle into some of its documents, such as 'Church and Land' (1980).

The base communities have also led the Church to rethink its position with regard to popular religiosity, and to open itself out to the most abandoned groups in society, who also have a right to have the faith handed on to them in a way that meets their needs and problems: 'The community should pay particular attention to and find the means of going out to meet the catechetical needs of those people whose condition of life makes it most difficult for them to participate in the normal life of the Christian community. We are thinking in particular of groups such as migrant workers, abandoned children, old people, long-distance truckers, shift workers, prisoners, prostitutes, tramps, etc.'.[6]

There are in the country some 100,000 Bible study groups and ecclesial base communities, all finding a new way of living the life of the Church and experiencing and handing on the faith. Some two and a half million people, from the popular classes, are involved in this project, whose most promising aspect is to be found in Jesus' reply to those sent by John the Baptist from prison: 'Go back and tell John what you hear and see . . . the Good News is proclaimed to the poor' (Matt. 11:4–5).

5. GROUP CATECHESIS AND MASS CATECHESIS

Beside the pastoral work of small groups and the base communities themselves, there is still a great challenge to be faced in the form of how to hand on the faith to the great mass of people who live beyond the reach of any network of communications, the anonymous men in the great cities, or young people who cannot find an answer to their problems either in their family, or school, or the traditional Church, or society in general.

One method that has been tried over the past twenty years is to try to involve the whole Church intensively in a campaign of mass evangelisation of the whole of society for a limited period on one particular topic. This has produced the 'Brotherhood Campaign' which is organised in Lent each year. Initially, the topics were rather intra-ecclesial: 'Be counted: you too are the Church' (1964). 'Make your parish a community of faith, worship and love' (1965). More recently the topics have been ones of general concern for society, such as unemployment and industrial injustice: 'Work and justice for all' (1978); or ecology: 'Look after what belongs to everyone' (1979); or migrant workers: 'Where are you going?' (1980); or health and brotherhood: 'Health for all' (1981), 'Brotherhood, Yes; Violence, No' (1983). Each topic has a theme, a slogan, a poster, a record with campaign songs, and is promoted through short advertisements on television. There is also a booklet with an introduction to the theme, liturgical services, ideas for prayer and reconciliation meetings, special texts for the Stations of the Cross and Holy Hour, services of reconciliation and outlines of catechetical approaches for use in parishes, schools and Bible study groups. Much of this material is quickly translated into more popular form, with illustrations and popular songs more suited to use in the base communities. Each campaign asks for practical actions, so that it has a real effect: the 'Work and Justice for all' campaign, for example, led the diocese of Lins to fight for the application and observance of the labour laws to domestic servants and casual labourers. In the ecology campaign, many groups mobilised to close polluting industrial plants, to have filters installed, or, in the worst places, to get piped water and a basic sewage system installed in the shanty towns. In the health campaign, many People's Health Committees were formed, teaching families basic household hygiene, campaigning to have health centres opened, to improve the staffing of government health centres and to denounce the precarious health conditions in which the majority of the people lived.

Less intense and widespread, but freer and more creative examples of catechesis and evangelisation, can be found in activities such as the Christmas novena. Taking up an element much loved by popular religiosity, novenas, this time has become a high point in community life, with often unexpected results. At the end of one such novena in Canoas no Rio Seco, a large group of shanty town families took over a huge area of land on the outskirts of the city, peaceably, as the beginning of a long struggle for land on which to live. Four years later the area houses 20,000 people, with nine community chapels/centres in which to meet and organise themselves, a creche, and a school. They have made the

Justice department give them the right to hold the land they occupy and the Prefecture supply them with water, electric light and drainage.

Another initiative worthy of note was the campaign of political education carried out by the Church at the time of the 1974 election, and intensified for the 1978 and 1982 elections, when, for the first time in twenty years, new political parties were organised and State Governors were elected by direct vote. The Church took on the task of political education as one of the dimensions and obligations of a militant faith. More than fifty pamphlets of political education and orientation were drawn up, in a popular style, over the whole country, some on a diocesan basis, some provincial, some regional or even national, such as that produced by the Commission for Pastoral Work on the Land, all of which served as a basis for discussion in small groups. The Church justified this undertaking by its understanding of the political dimension of preaching the Gospel. While refusing to apply its teaching to the aspirations of any one party, it declared that it was not a-political: 'It knows that a so-called a-politicism in practice means a political stance of tacit acquiescence in a particular form of political power, whatever it might be'.[7]

This involvement in the political dimension of life, and continual examination of this dimension in the light of the Gospel, with the consequent stress on reflection not being divorced from specific action, has had the effect for masses of people of giving their faith a consistency and relevance which till then only a few could achieve. It has also led to the birth of a theology committed to the cause and struggles of the poor, simpler, more closely linked to life and reality.

There is one particular element I should like to stress, which has played a most valuable role in the process of transformation which has led to a new ecclesial practice, in which faith and life are united, and to a new theoretical vision in which the theology of liberation has come together with a new form of organisation to produce the base communities: this is song.

6. SONG AND POPULAR CATECHESIS

At the time of the Protestant Reformation in the sixteenth century, what captivated and finally evangelised the masses was nothing to do with theological disputes and warring princely factions, but the evangelical hymnal. Till the middle of the nineteenth century, individual reading of the bible remained the prerogative of the more cultured sectors of the population. Just as in the middle ages, the gothic cathedrals, peopled with saints and episodes from the life of Jesus, unfolded a vast catechism of stone images before the eyes of pilgrims to Chartres, Santiago de Compostela or Rheims, so Luther's hymns moulded the souls of the German peasants. While the former were visually catechised through a panoply of images, the latter were orally catechised through song and the sound of the organ.

Something very similar is happening in Brazil today. Just as the hymnal catechised and re-educated the popular sectors of the European population in the sixteenth century, so, wherever base communities arise, new songs flourish, celebrating the struggles and hopes of a people organising itself and sowing the seeds of a new Church and a new society. There are hundreds of songs, most of them local, but gradually spread through meetings between different communities, copied out into notebooks, recorded on cassettes. Some have become known throughout the whole country and are always heard at particular celebrations. The songs of the communities have become the main vehicle for linking the realities of life to the events narrated in the Bible, using the language, rhythms and musical instruments of the people, rediscovering the Indian and African roots of the people in music.

This is a new aspect of the transmission of faith, succeeding in harnessing the power that only the feelings engendered by poetic form, melody and rhythm can impress on the human soul. The real re-encounter of the Church with the popular tradition is taking place in the songs of the communities. They have become the most valuable heritage in the process of handing the faith on to new generations, a patrimony equal in value to the Psalms for the Jewish people or the evangelical hymnal for the Churches that sprang from the Reformation.

I should like to give a few examples from these songs. From the Acre communities, written by a leper, comes a song firm in hope:

> I believe the world will be a better place
> When the suffering people trust in their race.

From Rio Grande do Norte comes a song rebelling against conformity:

> 'Set the poor people free', Jesus said—
> Christians must fight to give them bread.
> We are born to grow into life,
> Not for poverty, sorrow and strife.

From the Aragaia communities, where Fr John Bosco Burnier was murdered in cold blood when he went, with the bishop, to the prison at Ribeirão Bonito, where two women were being tortured, comes a song celebrating the destruction of the prison and the setting up of a cross where it stood:

> Ribeirão Bonito, the cross of Father John,
> Where the high walls stood, now the people march on,
> Where the soil is fed with your sweat and your blood . . .

From São Paulo, where Santo Dias da Silva, a community president and opposition metalworkers' union leader, was assassinated at his factory gate, comes a song of perseverance in the struggle:

> Santo, the fight will go on,
> Once more your words will resound
> As workers find common ground
> And your sons battle on . . .

There are also the 'hard' songs, echoing the prophets' maledictions on those who usurp the rights of the poor, the orphans, the widows, strangers:

> What you've got there . . .
> Your law and order, security forces
> Are the people's tears, their shattered hopes.

> What you've got there . . .
> Is the workers' blood, the hungry children,
> The sad eyes of the people over here—
> That's what you've got there . . .

Then there are songs expressing the hope that one day work will no longer be exploitation, but sharing and community among brothers, resurrecting the utopia of the poor:

Through the power of love let the world have pity
And the bright stars light my way,
In the springs of justice let my work be a sharing.
The orchards will blossom . . .
And in their fruit I shall pluck my freedom.

7. CHALLENGES FACING CATECHESIS

Beside the certainty that in the midst of the present troubles, ways are being opened up for a life of faith to be possible, and channels explored through which the faith can be handed on to the new generations, there are still some difficulties to be faced, such as the following:

—There is a whole generation of children and young people for whom television is their only companion for hours on end every day, who are bombarded with advertisements, images and concepts that have nothing to do with their own cultural heritage, since the majority of programmes they watch are canned North American imports.
—The Church, its message and the experience of the base communities is almost entirely absent from the world of video. Television passes on the images and societal models of a consumer society accessible to perhaps 20% of the Brazilian population, with the remaining 80% remaining beyond the reach of the models and values portrayed. The faith will not be handed on to future generations without taking account of the massive and decisive presence of TV in the cultural world of tomorrow.
—The world of tomorrow will be increasingly technical and scientific. Its patterns of thought and action, the new ethical questions about life, genetic control, the use of atomic power, the scientist's responsibility, etc., all derive from research centres and universities. Unfortunately, the existing Catholic universities of the country have not combined technical and scientific enquiry with theological reflection. Even the Pastoral University, the apple of the Church's eye in the 50s and 60s, has not managed to revitalise itself in this respect.
—Priestly formation in the last twenty years has left much to be desired in terms of depth of study and theoretical training, despite its open-mindedness in the pastoral field and its approach to political and social problems. European theology, till then taught in seminaries and theological institutes, has lost much of its relevance in the face of the reality of life in Brazil, and Latin American theology, despite its obvious advances in the fields of Christology, ecclesiology and even biblical theology, has equally obvious gaps in other fields.

Puebla, enumerating the challenges facing evangelisation and catechesis on the continent, lists three types of situation:

—Perduring situations: our indigenous peoples who are habitually left on the margins of life, and who are evangelised inadequately, or sometimes not at all; also the Afro-Americans, who are often forgotten.
—New situations, which arise from sociocultural changes and call for a new evangelisation: emigrants to foreign countries; human urban conglomerations in our countries; the masses in every social stratum whose faith-situation is precarious; and those most exposed to the influence of sects and ideologies that do not respect their identity and that provoke confusion and divisiveness.
—Particularly difficult situations: groups urgently in need of evangelisation that is often

postponed, such as university students, military people, labourers, young people, and those in the media of social communication. (365–367).

Puebla lists particularly difficult situations, new situations and 'perduring situations'. Among the latter are the Indians and the Afro-Americans. For these two groups, the Church has in the past not been able to escape from the contradictions inherent in presenting at one and the same time an evangelising face, bringing the good news of the gospel, and a colonial face, enslaving and bringing oppression and bad news. In some places, following the example of men like Las Casas in Spanish America or Vieira in Brazil, the Church has tried to fight against the enslavement of the Indians, but without being able to prevent their being made subject, removed from their tribes and made part of the colonial project. For the negroes, the colonial system and the slave system are indissolubly united and the Church never failed to provide the religious or ideological cement holding such political or social regimes together. This requires the Church to make a painful reexamination of its past and to take a courageous attitude in the present. With regard to the Brazilian Indians, CIMI (the Indigenous Missionary Council) has made concrete steps in the direction of a new type of evangelisation, which does not involve substituting a white culture for an indigenous one, nor the imposition of a new language, nor the destruction of old customs, feasts, ways of praying and of celebrating. In relation to the Blacks, the task is greater and the beginnings more rudimentary. Recognising the otherness of the Indians, their right to their own land, their own culture and their own forms of religious expression, which evangelisation must foster rather than destroy, is a process affecting some 200,000 people belonging to about a hundred different tribes. The Church's new approach to the Afro-Brazilian population, which it has neither catechised nor evangelised, involves nearly sixty million people, in whose veins runs the blood of their African inheritance and whose religious practice combines fidelity to the Church with adherence to their African origins.

Some steps taken in their direction, which stand out as signals to the conscience of the Church, have run into difficulties. I am thinking of two specially devised masses, the *Missa da Terra Sem Males* and the *Missa dos Quilombos*. The first takes up the mythic background of the Guarani peoples, who undertook great journeys in search of a land without evils (*sem males*), in which there would be neither suffering nor death. The poetry of Pedro Tierra and Pedro Casaldáliga was set to music by a native musician, who used the melodies and rhythms of his people. The second, written by the same two authors, evokes the villages to which slaves fled and the saga of their quest for liberation. The music is by one of our greatest black singers and composers, Milton Nascimento, and the mass was celebrated for the first time in Recife, on 20 November 1980, the day of Black Consciousness in Brazil.

Rome banned the celebration of both these masses in Brazil, on the grounds that the eucharistic celebration should be 'a solemn memorial of the Passion and Death of the Lord and not (trace) a revindication of any particular human or racial group.' Black revindication in Brazil concerns half the population and involves the memory of a people martyred by so-called Western Christian civilisation, a people in whose face Puebla invites us to see the face of Christ himself: 'This situation of pervasive extreme poverty takes on very concrete faces in real life. In these faces we ought to recognise the suffering features of Christ the Lord, who questions and challenges us. They include:

—the faces of the indigenous people, and frequently of the Afro-Americans as well; living marginalised lives in inhuman situations, they can be considered the poorest of the poor' (31, 34). In the passion and death of the Indians and Blacks of Brazil and Latin America, there is hidden the face of Christ, and in them the memorial of the Lord's death and Resurrection is kept alive, reactualised in the eucharist.

For Rome, however, not even the explanations sent by the auxiliary Bishop of Recife were sufficient: 'The account given by the auxiliary Bishop of Recife concerning the 'Missa dos Quilombos', which your Excellency openly refers to, while admirable in the zeal for repentance and reparation it demonstrates, cannot make this Dicastery refrain from pronouncing a judgement and not allowing, in the future, acts similar to this 'Missa dos Quilombos'.[8]

The catechesis of popular groups in the context of base communities led the Church in Brazil to produce a *Directory for Masses with Popular Groups* in 1977. This for the first time went beyond mere translation and adaptation for the popular levels of what had been produced by a learned and lettered cultural group for a different, unlettered and uncultured group. It included the right of the popular groups to produce their own liturgical celebrations, to find their own rites and actions, to use their own songs, their own tradition, rhythms, musical instruments and linguistic tradition, which expresses itself more in dialogue than in the written word. This *Directory*, produced with the approval of the bishops of Brazil in 1977, in accordance with the new practice and commitments of the Church in Brazil, provoked a vigorous response from Rome, forbidding its implementation, on the grounds that it would prove a danger 'to the future durability of the Roman Rite'.[9]

For the future of catechesis in a country like Brazil, it is vital that ways be kept open for improving communication between the Gospel and the culture of the people, between the Word of God and the country's Indian and African heritage. This makes it equally vital that misguided campaigns against the Church of the people should not be allowed to hinder the growth of the base communities, this 'new way of being Church', the central thrust of the current rediscovery and handing on of faith.

Translated by Paul Burns

Notes

1. *Comunidades Eclesiais de Base no Igreja do Brasil* CNBB Doc. 25 (São Paulo 1982).
2. A Antoniazzi 'Revelação de Catequese' in *Rev. de Cat.* 6, 24 (Oct–Dec. 1983) 20.
3. *Catequese renovada—Orientações e Conteúdo* 120, 1983.
4. Puebla, no. 1174.
5. *CEBs no Igreja do Brasil*, the work cited in note 1, 63.
6. *Catequese renovada* 143.
7. 'Reflexão cristã sobre a conjuntura política', Doc. of the Permanent Council, no. 6 (1981).
8. Letter from the Sacred Congregation for the Sacraments and Divine Worship to Most Rev. Ivo Lorscheiter (Rome, 2 Mar. 1982) no. 1649/81. (Published in the Monthly Communiqué of the Bishops' Conference, March 1982, p. 258.)
9. Letter from the same congregation, signed by Cardinal James Knox, to Most Rev. Ivo Lorscheiter, President of the Brazilian Bishops' Conference, dated 4 Dec. 1979, pub. in CELAM *Bulletin* 145, year XIII, no. 145, Jan. 1980, pp. 16–17.

Gerard Vogeleisen

Catechesis: Handing on the Faith Today

HOW CAN the Church make its message heard, and get it listened to, in the secularised and post-industrial world we now inhabit? How, in particular, can it do this among the rising generations, the children and young people born into this new world and so no longer sharing the habits of thought and the culture on which education in the Church used to rely?

Formulated so generally, the question inevitably produces vague, disappointing and partial answers. Its main failing is precisely treating the socio-cultural situation in general, when one of the dominant characteristics of that situation is that it presents itself as diverse and fragmented. This sort of language, which abstracts from the situation in which the message of faith is uttered, also implies that there is no need to distinguish between the message and the situation.

The alternative approach is to concentrate on a few specific aspects of a particular situation, on the assumption that the analyses will not only be more precise but also, *mutatis mutandis*, more easily transposable to other situations. This is my reason for hoping that these few notes on the development of catechesis in France may be of interest, even outside their specific context, and may encourage others to examine their own situations.

I shall tackle the question in three stages. First, what position can the Church find for itself in a fragmented world such as we experience today in France? Second, does the experience of catechetics in the recent past indicate dead ends and useful routes? What are the ways forward suggested by current analysis?

1. A FRAGMENTED WORLD, AN IDENTITY TO BE FOUND

There is no need to build up here a detailed picture of this changing world. There is no lack of relevant descriptions, analyses and controversies. A convenient summary of the main features of the situation was produced in 1979 by the French bishops' conference.[1]

'The fragmentation of the world' and 'cultural change' are frequently heard phrases. The universe in which the generations who form the adult world were brought up and have lived their lives had a different structure from the world in which their children are developing. . . . Reference to generally accepted values, some of which were considered universal in our Western philosophy, enabled people to find a degree of stability. . . .

Some of these values, so important for the society of yesterday, are now being challenged at their very roots, and not simply by fashionable ideologies, but by everyday life. The universe of our contemporaries . . . is riven by movements which question previously accepted principles. . . . If life has a meaning, it now seems to be less something written on the face of the world than something which has to be discovered among the many interpretations of reality, and even in their discord (RT 121).

Family, school and church, all are marked by this context. 'In some areas . . . unbelief is total. The ideas of God, religion, the meaning of life have lost all meaning, to the point where they are no longer mentioned. . . . In a pluralist world marked by concern for efficiency and the demands of production the Church no longer has the same visibility (RT 124). It is in this context that catechesis in France is developing' (RT 13).

This diagnosis does point to signs of hope, but they cannot obscure the consequences of the change.

The French Church no longer has the same social visibility, and it can no longer have the same influence. The loss of this influence began earlier than is usually thought. The separation of the churches and the State in 1905 led, almost inevitably, in a few generations, to a privatisation of faith and its institutional expressions. While not absent from public life, the Church's political influence is generally not obtrusive. Free from official, institutional or financial support, the Church has no other base to rely on than the credence which public opinion gives or withholds. As everyday life becomes secularised, the Church's 'moral' and ethical influence on the majority of the population is declining, despite being, here and there, the object of disparate and confused expectations.

As regards the values of life and its meaning, the Church has lost not only the monopoly it used to enjoy, but also its former dominant influence.

Even the 'religious sense'

Even more recently, almost before our eyes, a non-rational upsurge has appeared to complicate the picture. One of its forms, a 'return of religion', usually para-Christian or derived from Asian sources, has brought a nostalgic comfort to some Christians. The reality, however, is that, confronted with these burgeoning beliefs, these wild-cat religions, often mainly emotional, the Church becomes aware of something else that it has lost: to some extent, the 'religious sense' itself has slipped out of its control. Now anyone can open up shop in religion or mysticism; the market is not saturated, contrary to what many people thought about thirty years ago.

The market is not saturated, and it is not even regulated any more. All sorts of competing offers are available, but none of them has the status of an ultimate adversary. In this fragmented universe the Church cannot even find its unity in resolute opposition to a main antagonist.

Among this host of challengers, the Church faces one whose varied and growing influence is well matched to the 'crisis of values and meaning' which affects us. Considered or spontaneous, assertive or hesitant, passionate or resigned, religious indifference meets every message with a calm refusal, a 'spiritual torpor', a disenchanted absence of search for meaning.[2]

On top of this, even within its own ranks the community of believers no longer feels itself to be monolithic. Political and social opinions, moral positions, dogmatic positions and religious attitudes too often divide Christians within a single Church. This may go to the extreme of open conflict, though it more often remains within the silence of personal conviction and behaviour. The number of 'half-believers', in the Church or on its edges, is increasing. Among them in particular the temptation to indifference is strong.

This is the context in which the word must be proclaimed and Christian identity established (RT 2212, CT 56, 57),[3] in which ecclesial communion must be made visible. It presents the Church with a challenge.

A swift review of the recent history of catechesis will perhaps indicate why some people in the Church have been taken unawares by this situation, and may explain many of the hesitations and tensions. It will also indicate ways forward.

2. A LITTLE HISTORY

(a) A single catechism

Until after the Council the official French catechism was a textbook in the classical mould, using a question and answer method to present systematically the totality of the truths of faith (dogma, morals and the sacraments). It was produced in 1937 and revised in 1947, and is rich in material from dogmatics, moral theology and canon law. Its language is conceptual and abstract, and in places the presentation barely conceals an outdated apologetics.

There is no doubt that the classical model on which this book is based had its value and was effective at a time when its function was to instruct the Christian and to help him or her 'to formulate the faith they lived and saw lived day by day' (RT 2112). Despite its rigidity and its tendency to apportion blame,[4] it was undeniably a factor for humane education and social integration, particularly under the *ancien régime*.

This catechism presents and defines the meaning of existence by means of a deduction which starts from fixed essences attributed to God, man and things. Each element of the world, object, value or person, derives its existence from its vertical constitutive relation to the divine model. In such a mentality catechesis sees its aim as transmitting this Christian meaning of life and regards this as adequately expressed by definitions of absolute essences.

Time and changes in outlook have revealed the weaknesses of this approach, weaknesses which are the mirror images of its strengths. Its abstraction keeps it remote from everyday experience and creates a language and outlook detached from the surrounding world. A gulf opens up between 'faith' and 'life'.[5]

Settling into what they took to be the truth, Catholics ceased to question themselves about their own standpoint. Little by little, the Church gave a privileged, an absolute, position to a single way of looking at things. It seemed to raise itself above the contingencies of history and the limits of culture; even revelation's roots in human history were obscured. Trapped in its Church-centred world, it lost the ability to judge other points of view in any other way than by measuring their difference from its own. The Church came to think of itself as the sole centre of the human universe and the exclusive trustee of the meaning of life. Faced with questions from outside, it regarded a hardening of old positions as a sufficient response.

Of course, gaps appeared in this monolithic construction, but nostalgia for the old certainties remained strong. The Church had created an expression of the faith admirably adapted to the 'essentialist' culture of a period, and to its political and cultural mechanisms. The disadvantage was that, having become welded to a particular age,[6] the faith proved hard to detach from that age as it slipped into the past. A telling indication of this is the fact that the classical manuals remained current until 1966. The 'kerygmatic movement', whatever its indirect influence, did not generate a decisive phase here comparable to the one through which Germany passed in the 1950s. It was the impulse of the council which made the change possible and encouraged an 'anthropological switch' by giving official sanction to much of the work done by the catechetical movement.

C

(b) Anthropological catechesis

The years 1966–1970, the euphoric aftermath of the Council, brought an important reform. Catechesis rediscovered the great tradition and turned its attention back to those who were called to hear the message and respond to it. Starting from a central document, 'adaptations' were produced for different socio-religious backgrounds. The same process generated the idea of a 'pedagogy of signs', a route which went from the visible signs of revelation, scripture, liturgy, tradition and church life—and from ordinary life—to an unfolding of their meaning, to awaken and nourish faith.

By its attention to people's real experience, this interpretation was intended to bridge the gulf between 'faith' and 'life'. With its rediscovery of the emphases of biblical and liturgical language, the message shifted to centre on the mystery of Christ and the life of the Church; every human reality was to discover its 'Christian meaning'. The community of believers, the group which had undergone the catechesis, were now able to become once more a sign of the Word of God.

It may be felt that, with the weakening of the reactive energy which powered it at that time, 'anthropological' catechetics has on occasions become impoverished in comparison with its sources and its early strength. The desire to 'adapt' the message brings with it three risks. First, the interpretation of existence may stay at the level of behaviour and faith may be reduced to trivial moralising. Second, the 'Christian meaning', which is presented as the only possible one, comes to seem an addition, something superfluous or relying on an undue preoccupation with the Church. Third, the radical otherness of the word of God and of the mystery revealed in it is in danger of being diluted into a mere divine benevolence.

Conversely, these dangers show very clearly that the gulf between 'faith' and 'life' has not been bridged. The anthropocentrism which might have liberated catechists twenty years previously is no longer equal to interpreting 'life' in the seventies and eighties. On the one hand, ignoring the findings of the human sciences, this tendency does not see clearly enough the connections between a truth, a human meaning and the language and structures which give them expression or the complexities of the history and culture in which they are expressed. On the other hand, making too great a separation between the faith as a set of organised truths and faith as a human response, as a human vision of the mystery of God in Jesus Christ, breaks its fundamental unity. Finally, it obscures the fact that this faith has an original, primordial setting, the believing community with its life and celebration.

Initiated by the *Reference Text*, the new stage of catechetics is attempting something bolder in serenely accepting cultural change; but it is also less ambitious and limits its sights to the next ten years.

3. THE CONTEXTS FOR CATECHESIS

To leave the old certainties behind without regret and to nourish one's faith in an encounter with the new culture: this is the challenge. In accepting it, catechesis finds a direction and a route in this new country in which it knows that it is a fragile minority. Its only possible starting point is the present profession of faith, its only goal the profession of faith of the Church which is to come. Between the two there is an experience of ecclesial life.

(a) From profession of faith to profession of faith

Starting from the message of the 1977 synod, the bishops note that catechesis is rooted in the profession of faith of a community and journeys towards the profession of faith within the Church (RT 2111). It cannot exist without communities within which the catechised can have an experience of life within the Church (RT 1322). This is the source of the bishops' desire to create settings which make this experience possible. These are the contexts of catechesis (RT 2113).

Bringing these contexts to life does not mean renewing the catechism classes by redrawing area boundaries, but making use of a time of movement during which encounter and experience are possible,[7] offering a *space* in which, in the encounter, relations can be formed between the persons and the word, offering a specific setting for experience. In addition to a 'content', which in isolation always tends to abstraction, to becoming a closed ideology, the emphasis is on time and relationships.[8]

Finally, aware of a process of becoming, this approach allows for the unpredictability of the particular forms and new shapes Christianity will take in a culture being constructed along side it.

(b) The mystery of Christ and revelation

Theologically, this option is based on two theses, the mystery of Christ and revelation. Because of Jesus Christ, in whom dwells the fulness of the mystery of God, Christian universality is never abstract, rationalised, made uniform, but specific, situated, rooted. Jesus' particular rootedness in humanity guarantees the particular value of our own rootedness—and its openness to the universal. Because of this an abstract catechesis will always be inadequate.

Moreover, Jesus can be met and recognised as the Christ only through the time of the witnesses who testify to us on his behalf, and in affiliation to the Church which confesses him. Revelation is history, not merely a deposit, but also an appeal and a promise. In it we hear the word of God in so far as it lights up our existence and enables it to become our history of salvation. In this sense revelation has constantly to be created, as an acceptance of particularities, as the structuring of a significant experience and as an appeal to conversion. This now is the task of catechesis.

Christological reflection also makes it easier to answer the recurrent question of the content of catechesis. Since the mystery of Christ is its centre, the content of any catechesis must have to do with attachment to the person of Christ (John 20:30–31). Through the story and the experience of the witnesses, this attachment takes place in the profession of faith within a community. The content is therefore inseparable from the experience of believers through the ages, and the task of catechetics is to integrate scripture and tradition in its work as primary and exemplary experiences.[9]

(c) Languages and pedagogies

The idea that there is an isolable content which languages have to express and methods of education to 'put across' loses much of its force against this background. Words are never neutral, and every language divides up reality in its own way; at the same time every language induces a particular way of thinking. Languages, methods, pedagogies and institutions are not just simple tools; they are structures of mediation and themselves create an element of meaning.

When, for example, catechesis is imparted magisterially by a cleric in a place set apart for the purpose, its message is not the same as when it is decentralised to familiar surroundings, in small groups led by lay people, with active methods which stimulate response. The revelation of God to man is not uttered in the same way in the two situations. The experience of faith evoked as a response is not the same, nor is the image of the Church.

A 'Christian meaning' developed through a pedagogy of signs, stories and evidence will not be the same as one presented ready-made, to be repeated. The conditions of production necessarily form part of the meaning; though it was not the first to say so, our culture is repeating this to us. That is why the only meaning which will be valid is one constructed, even though with difficulty and inexactly, from experience. The risk of this precarious venture is where freedom has to prove itself today.

(d) Contexts of acceptance and verification

To make such an experience possible, the catechetical context must be one in which differences are accepted and relationships valued. 'It is a context in which the life-experiences of different people are taken into account, in which the deep desires and the aspirations of the participants are given a value in their own right, where the Good News of Jesus Christ is expressed in function of the life of each person, in which the testimony of all those it brings together—directors, parents and children—allows a real sharing of faith' (RT 3111).

In this context each person welcomes the Word of God, which is always greater than they. Each person is called by his or her own name, since between the gift and the promise of God announced in the different books of the Bible and the profession of faith, 'there remains a place to be continually filled by the reader, according to what the Spirit suggests to him or her' (RT 2223). Each person is confronted with the Gospel, and also with the other members of the group. This confrontation is a condition of the truth of the welcome. Only difference, otherness, can lead to the break of conversion, and only this break can lead a person to a 'reappraisal' of their faith, in which the believer no longer builds himself up, but receives himself, coming back to the experience of the Church.

Catechesis does not try to jump stages. It works through differences and takes the time it needs. The task it sets itself is to teach those being catechised to give a structure to this meaning of existence by examining experiences and facing difference. The functional aim which catechesis sets itself could be said to be to educate people for this work of articulation. In a world dominated by the 'crisis of meaning', and sometimes by a forgetfulness of history and a neglect of mediations, work is not lacking. The venture is a bold one, but success is quite possible. In this way, starting from the ecclesial impulse which gave it birth, catechesis is contributing to 'making the Church', to building a Church capable of giving an account of its faith in the language of its time.

4. A FINAL WORD

Diversity is without doubt one of the most striking characteristics of French catechetics, diversity of settings, resources, people, inspirations, workers, methods. An account as short as this cannot hope to do justice to this diversity, and must just sketch the main lines.

It would also be a mistake to see this work as taking place only within catechetical institutions. Other bodies and other movements are engaged in it, albeit with different understandings. The work of catechesis is inseparable from the mission of the Church and crosses institutional boundaries.

From the number of projects and their diversity it will be clear that catechesis cannot be reduced, today less than ever, to catechism for children and young people. To form the greatest possible number of responsible Christians in the Church is the main aim of the venture on which the 'catechetical contexts' have embarked. The transmission of the faith to tomorrow's generation begins with the formation of today's adults.

At the same time it would be incorrect to say that the direction taken by the *Reference Text* has been accepted unanimously. Some question the terms of the venture; active minorities oppose it. Declared, muffled, or conducted behind the scenes, conflicts are being joined, and for the moment the discussion is not closed.[10] Only the future will tell how far real commitment will go to folow up the bishops' courageous collegial decision.

An ecclesial faith

In addition to this survey of the changing historical scene, I wish to make three final points.

(*i*) If our contemporaries have to make their act of faith in uncertainty and a sense of the 'absence of God', an analysis of the process of belief needs to sharpen its distinction between the personal act of believing, the community's profession of faith and the regulations of the *magisterium*. Distinguishing these three expressions does not mean dissociating them, but bringing about an effective interaction between them, so that each can find its place in relation to the others and enter into a fruitful dialogue with them. Catechists encounter this problem when they bring together a group in which they hope to see and foster a living cell of the emerging Church.

(*ii*) Led by its sacramental dimension, catechesis today is giving new emphasis to the unexpectedness and gratuitousness of God's gift. In the personal and social structures of the past it often polarised faith by an idea of certainty, unity and utility which was meant to give security. Today we seem to be at a crossing of the ways. Catechesis can reformulate these old securities in currently fashionable language, and some people ask no more of it than that.

Alternatively, it may choose dispossession and precariousness, and acquire a new lease of life in the language and attitude of gratitude, thanksgiving and celebration. The emphasis shifts from what we 'hold' to what we 'receive'. Like faith itself, the transmission of the Christian message is then seen primarily as a free gift given to the disciples in the word of the Son and the breath of the Spirit (Matt. 28:18–20; Mark 16:20). Moved by gratitude, catechesis responds to this gift in the silences and the languages of its time.

(*iii*) In the context of pastoral work as a whole, catechesis in France takes its place, more or less deliberately, in between evangelisation and sacramentalisation: it addresses those who have been converted in order to lead them to the sacraments and a fuller Christian life. This model has been transposed rather rapidly from Christian antiquity to the institutions of our time. Is it not in need of revision now that 'conversion' covers the whole span of existence, and 'catechetical contexts' are welcoming people whose age, maturity, 'conviction of faith' and 'degree of sacramentalisation' are no longer in any sense homogeneous?

Translated by Francis McDonagh

Notes

1. French Bishops' Conference, Lourdes 1979. *La Catéchèse des enfants. Texte de réference au service des auteurs de publications catéchétiques et des responsables de la pastorale* (Paris 1980). Cited here as RT (Reference Text).

2. For interesting interpretations see *Concilium* 165 (1983) and *L'Indifférence religieuse* (*Le Point Théologique* 41) (Paris 1983).

3. CT: *Catechesi Tradendae* Apostolic Exhortation of 16 October 1979, *AAS* LXXI (1979) 1277–1340, English translation: *Apostolic Exhortation Catechesi Tradendae of Pope John Paul II*, C.T.S., London.

4. See J. Delumeau *Le Péché et la peur. La cuplabilisation en Occident (XIIIe–XVIIIe siècles)* (Paris 1983). The power to inspire fear is one element of its influence.

5. It is not the systematic presentation which is being questioned here, but the system of presentation. The *Credo* is a profession of faith. The French bishops comment on a eucharistic prayer to proclaim the faith (Lourdes 1978). On 'completeness' in presentations of the Christian mystery, see CT 21.

6. See Y. Congar *Christianisme comme foi et comme culture, Evangelizzazione e culture, Atti del Congresso internazionale scientifico di Missiologia* (Rome 1976) I, 83–103.

7. The experience mentioned here is not pure spontaneity or immediacy; it is re-examination, re-reading, reinterpretation. See P. Jacquemont, J.-P. Jossua, B. Quelquejeu *Une Foi exposée* (Paris 1972) pp. 171–174; A. Godin *Psychologie des expériences religieuses* (Paris 1981) *passim*; or G. Adler, G. Vogeleisen *Un Siècle de catéchèse en France* (Paris 1981) pp. 381–400.

8. This paragraph and the following one draw largely on C. Cesbron 'Les Lieux catéchétiques' *Catéchèse* 85 (1981) 9–19.

9. *Ibid*. 18.

10. See G. Alder 'La Catéchèse: où est le problème?', *Etudes* 358 (June 1983) 829–843.

PART II

What Faith Are We to Transmit?

Johannes van der Ven

The Future of the Church as an Intergenerative Problem

DOES THE Church still have a future? This question, which occupies a central position in this article, cannot be swept aside by appealing to the Church's apostolic nature and the indestructibility that results from this (Matt. 16:18), to its necessity for salvation (*Lumen gentium* 14) or to the Spirit who 'perpetually renews' the Church (*Lumen gentium* 4) and brings it to fulfilment (*Lumen gentium* 2). The unease that is discernible in this question can also not be dismissed as a sin against the Spirit. The Spirit is, after all, only active in the Church in the activity of people. He is not active outside or above them, but at the same time his activity is not absorbed into that of people. There is, then, a surplus on the side of the Spirit, although that surplus is only given form in human activity, without being exhausted by that activity. We have therefore to accept responsibility for the future of the Church. It is a responsibility that is, because of that surplus of the Spirit to which I have referred and which is a surplus of grace, characterised by hope—often a hope against despair. This provides us with a basis for an empirical theological approach to the question of the future of the Church.

In this article, my point of departure for my approach to this question is the concept of *socialisation*, which I would define here as the *transfer of systems of meaning and values within the Church by one generation to the next*, in such a way that the latter is ready and able to hand on what it has received to the following generation. The tradition that comes about in this way within the Church therefore has, as one of its functions, the task of improving the cognitive, ethical, spiritual, liturgical, orthopractical and institutional aspects of Christian faith. There is also always tension between the maintenance of meaning and value-systems, which is present in all processes of socialisation, and changes in those systems and improvement only comes about when maintenance and change go together. Both primary and secondary socialisation are included in the process of socialisation and both aspects have a bearing on Church socialisation in and through the family and the school. In this article, I shall try to answer the question as to whether the view expressed about socialisation in the apostolic adhortation *Catechesi Tradendae* of 1979 (abbreviated to *CT* in this article) guarantees the future of the Church. I shall also include in this consideration the document *Evangelii Nuntiandi* of 1976 (abbreviated here to *EN*), since, according to *CT*, in which there are frequent references to *EN*, catechesis should be regarded as a part of evangelisation (see *CT* 18).

I propose to consider the process of socialisation in the Church according to five models. These can be situated in a continuum revealing both a decreasing maintenance and an increasing change in the meaning and value-systems of Christianity and the institutional basis of those systems in the Church. The fundamental question can therefore be summarised as what is the relationship between *CT* and *EN* and these five models and what is the significance of this for the future of the Church?

1. THE INCORPORATION MODEL

This model is directed towards handing down unchanged the meaning and value-system of the Church and its institutional basis in the Church to following generations in such a way that they can identify themselves completely with them. This model has a central position in *CT*, although it is not exclusive. The document states that the aim of catechesis is initiation into the fullness of the Christian life that is given form in complete participation in the community of the Church (*CT* 18). This initiation must be complete and it must also include all the aspects of Christian life (*CT* 21). Hence the constant emphasis in the document on the intactness of the Church's teaching in catechesis (*CT* 17, 26, 30). In this, the document follows the idea of *plena incorporatio* outlined in the Constitution on the Church of Vatican II (*Lumen gentium* 14).

Two objections can be raised against this incorporation model. The first is connected with Dilthey's view, which was later refined by Mannheim, that the concept of generation contained in every model of socialisation automatically includes the notion of change. Different generations ascribe a different meaning, even in the Church, to the same processes and structures in which they participate at the same moment, because they participate in them in the light of a different structure of biographical experience. This change is not discounted in the incorporation model, with the result that the very tension that it aims to suppress is produced.

The second objection is that the Church is situated in the midst of other social institutions that are similarly trying to transfer meaning and value-systems of their own to later generations. The Church is in a weak competitive position compared with these institutions in the economic, political and cultural sphere, which are concerned with science, technology, education, leisure time, art and so on. At the beginning of the present century, Max Weber pointed to fundamental discrepancies between the meaning and value-systems of the Church on the one hand and those of economic and political institutions on the other. More recently, Habermas has also pointed out that man's environment is becoming more and more colonised by economics and politics. It should therefore be clear that the idea of total identification which is at the heart of the incorporation model has no value as reality. *CT* has therefore to be criticised here too. It does not consider seriously a partial identification as a natural reaction to the competitive position of the Church in society. The need for cognitive and affective assimilation of competitive rôle expectations on the part of social institutions, including the Church, is not even discussed, nor is the need for role conflict and reflective role distance. In this respect, *CT* is obviously characterised by a closed socialisation model. It is outside the socially defined reality of the Church. There is simply no analysis of that reality. What is left in the document is well intentioned and even quite inspiring moralism, which is, however, unaware of what is taking place in the Church as a socially conditioned institution. This closed socialisation model of incorporation has no future, nor can it provide a future for the Church. This can be expressed rather paradoxically in the following way: The Church socialises young people, according to this model, out of the Church!

2. THE ADAPTATION MODEL

According to this model, the relevant meaning and value-systems and their institutional foundation in the Church are supplemented by adaptation to the demands made by changed circumstances and the way in which they are presented is adjusted. There is, then, a combination of accidental additions and cosmetic operations at the institutional level and at that of content. This and the incorporation model are the two that occur most frequently in *CT*.

What, then, are the changed circumstances that make this adaptation necessary? According to *CT*, they are not social, but connected with the psychology of development, with the result that they take place independently of the social context. This a-social understanding, which takes as its point of departure the psychology of human development, is, moreover, based on a non-empirical anad essentially speculative idea of a development through typical phases (see *CT* 35) of the cultural puberty of the early part of this century (see *CT* 38, 39). Seen in this perspective, a catechetical treatment of such social themes as work, justice, peace and liberation is regarded as supplementing a catechesis that is above all concerned with religious questions. The primacy of the Church's religious task, in which *CT* (39) closely follows *EN* (34), therefore leads to a dichotomy between the religious and the social aspects. Underlying this dichotomy is a religious and personalistic view of man, which gives a purely accidental significance to society and social changes— this emerges quite clearly, for example, in *CT* 38. The essential question, then, is whether this adaptation model, which is explicitly named in *CT* 42, is derived from a philosophical rather than a theological understanding of man and his faith and, what is more, from a philosophical understanding that has been superseded by an empirical approach especially in those points already mentioned.

3. THE REFORM MODEL

This model can be seen as situated between maintenance and change. It aims to reform both the content and the institution. It is conscious of the need to change both the traditional systems of meaning and values and the traditional institutional forms of those systems in such a way that justice is done to the intention of the Gospel and the Church in accordance with that Gospel in critical correlation with contemporary history and society. Catechesis according to this model means that those who are being catechised have to be initiated into this process of reform and given the task of continuing it.

Before I try to answer the question as to whether this reform model is discussed in *CT* and *EN* and, if it is discussed, how it is interpreted, I must first look more closely at the model itself. The question, then, that has to be answered first is: What are the contemporary history and society with which the Gospel and the Church in accordance with that Gospel have to brought into critical correlation? In the context of this article, I shall take as my point of departure the phenomenon of secularisation which has characterised the West for several centuries and which is already penetrating into the Third World. Despite this fact, however, the Church has only comparatively recently become aware of secularisation and it was not until the promulgation of *Gaudium et spes* by Vatican II that it was explicitly treated, *EN* is conscious of this phenomenon, but *CT* is marked by a certain regression. (This will be made clear later in this article.)

The central question, however, is: What is secularisation? In all the discussion that has taken place about the answer to this question and even about the question itself, two levels of conceptualisation can be distinguished. At the level of the superficial structure, secularisation means the reduced influence of religion and the Church on personal and social life. At the deeper level, secularisation is the result of the increasing rationalisation of personal and social life. I would like to discuss this process of increasing rationalisation in greater detail.

According to Weber, it is an irreversible process, but, according to Habermas, it can be corrected and guided. Purely instrumental rationality, Habermas believes, can be extended to include a three-dimensional rationality, the three aspects being instrumental, normative and expressive. This process of increasing rationality also has two characteristics, each of which must be briefly considered separately.

The first characteristic of increasing rationalisation is institutional pluralisation, resulting in an increasing ramification of society into separate, autonomous institutions which develop according to rational bureaucratic laws. One consequence of this compartmentalisation is that the Church has lost and is still losing its uniformative function and is becoming just one social institution among many others. It also means that it is becoming increasingly concentrated on the task that distinguishes it institutionally from other institutions. This makes it possible to understand why *CT* and *EN* stress the primacy of the religious task (see Section 2 above) and it also justifies that emphasis. It does not, however, mean, in my opinion at least, that the Church should disregard activities that are not directly religious. On the contrary, those activities should be legitimated on the basis of the Church's primarily religious task, although this might be, for the time being, utopian rather than realistic. Consciousness of institutional pluralisation has also resulted in the Church's explicit encounter with the phenomenon that two other kinds of institutions are also concerned with man's religious life—other Christian churches and other religions. This phenomenon has thrown the Church back on itself and has confronted it with other questions. The content of the Church's primarily religious task, which has just been considered, is not the only question now. Equally important is: How does the Church, in so far as this religious task is concerned, differ from these two other kinds of institutions? And perhaps an even more difficult question: What is the significance of the Church's universal nature?

Alongside and connected with this first characteristic of increasing rationalisation is a second feature: the process of desacralisation, by which the giving of religious meaning by men within and outside the Church has been and is being increasingly replaced by a giving of rational meaning to persons, things, structures and processes. The question that arises here is: How should the Church react to this? Does it accept the challenge of rationality fully and is it regarding every zone that is sheltered from the storms of reason as belonging to the past? Is it destroying all the notices announcing 'no access' to revelation itself and has it ceased to call for a *sacrificium intellectus*? Or is it still withdrawing, when things become difficult, into a fundamentalism or a fideism based on the Bible and/or the Church's *magisterium*?

If, with the first of these characteristics in mind, we turn to *CT* and *EN*, then it is apparent that there is no trace of the general phenomenon of institutional pluralisation in the two documents and that *CT* is extremely cautious with regard to the two other kinds of institutions that are concerned with man's religious life. This can be elaborated as follows. Referring to the Catholic Church's relationship with other Christian churches, *CT* states, following the teaching of Vatican II (*Lumen gentium* 8), that the fullness of salvation is encountered in the Catholic Church (*CT* 32). Following the Decree on Ecumenism (*Unitatis redintegratio* 3), the other churches are positively assessed as means of salvation (*CT* 32), but the Catholic Church is presented as the universal means of salvation and the document insists that it ought also to be presented as such in catechesis (*CT* 32). What is lacking in *CT*, but is encountered in *EN* (77), where the teaching of Vatican II is followed, is the recognition that the division between the churches implies a serious weakening of the effectiveness of the transference of faith from one generation to the next. This division is called a 'stumbling block to the world' in the Decree on Ecumenism (*Unitatis redintegratio* 1). Seen from the point of view of socialisation, there is no doubt that the future of the

Church itself is in the long run seriously endangered when it is no longer possible to explain what is separating the churches and why the Catholic Church clings so firmly to its own structure to younger generations. Following Vatican II (*Unitatis redintegratio* 11), the future of the Church is furthered by a 'hierarchy of truths'—a *hierarchia veritatum ecclesiologiae catholicae*. In view of the fact that this *ecclesiologia catholica* occupies a secondary position within the *doctrina catholica*, I would suggest that what is of secondary importance in that *ecclesiologia catholica* itself should be thrown into the crucible of an ecumenical reinstitutionalisation of the Church. In other words, the contemporary Catholic Church is really standing in the way of its own future.

CT is also very reserved in its attitude towards other religions. Manuals introducing the different religions, among which is included the Catholic—not the Christian!—religion, are regarded as important by *CT* in so far as they contain objective information, but they cannot be accepted as catechetical works (*CT* 34). The reasons for this are that they lack the testimony of believers and an understanding of the Christian mysteries and the distinctive character of the Catholic (*sic!*). In my opinion, what is under review in this instance is not the catechetical or non-catechetical character of these manuals, but rather their educative or non-educative character. After all, books which aim to introduce readers to different religions must, from the didactic and educational point of view, contain both hetero and auto-interpretations of those religions. On that basis, dialogue between the various religions must be conducted and that is precisely what is lacking in *CT* and in *EN*, although, unlike *CT*, *EN* expresses the Church's respect for other religions (*EN* 53). The absence of dialogue is, of course, understandable in view of the Church's claim to universality, a claim which makes dialogue intrinsically impossible. I have myself personally experienced the fact that a public statement of doubt regarding the legitimacy of that claim by representatives of other religions is regarded as an indication of superiority and imperialism. It is tragic that the claim to universality, which the Church refuses to discuss in dialogue with other religions, no longer forms a discussion point for future generations and furthermore is frequently introduced as an argument against the credibility of the Church. Research has shown that the enlightened consciousness of a Lessing regarding the equal value of religions has become less in the case of many ordinary people and that anyone who is 'enlightened' by a rational upbringing and rational education tends to abandon the Church's claim to universality and also the Church that makes such a claim.

Let us now, with the second characteristic, that of desacralisation, in mind, consider the two documents, *CT* and *EN*. Are there any traces of this in *CT*? Secularisation in the sense of desacralisation does in fact occur in a few places in *CT*, but, wherever it does, it is found in extremely short affirmative statements (see, for example, *CT* 42 and 44) or expressed in terms of defensive strategy. This defensive strategy consists of two elements, the first of which is the formation of those receiving catechesis in such a way that they are strengthened and able to persevere in faith in a secularised world (57). The second element is family catechesis, that is, catechesis in the small church of the family as the only environment in which children and young people still receive authentic catechesis (68). This is suggested in the document as though it really corresponds with the empirical reality and is able to keep the process of secularisation away from the family! Even more important, this defensive strategy offers no scope to the model of critical correlation, which we must now briefly consider.

The model of critical correlation is based on two data. The first is the obvious fact that the Christian consciousness of transcendence has disappeared. This does not, however, mean that all consciousness of transcendence has disappeared without a trace! Contemporary man is always making efforts to be raised above everyday experience and to gain an insight into the ultimate meaning of reality and he does again and again have such transcendent experiences. According to the model of critical correlation, the meaning and value-systems of the Christian tradition should be placed within this sphere of human experiences of transcendence, thus making it possible for connections to be established between them. These connections have, of course, to be established in a differentiated manner. The significance of these human experiences of transcendence can be emphasised, relativised, supplemented, criticised or corrected in the light of the Christian tradition. The defensive strategy of *CT* clearly offers no scope for this model of critical correlation to be developed, but fortunately this is not the case with *EN*, which refers to the need to establish authentic links between secularisation and Christianity despite mutual criticism (55). The earlier document speaks of the need to find the right language for the proclamation of faith in the secularised world (56) and especially in catechesis (63). Language is understood in *EN* in the anthropological and cultural sense rather than in the semantic sense (63), the task being seen as the 'inculturation' of the Christian faith into contemporary culture and society. The theme of the 'signs of the times' is also mentioned with remarkable frequency in *EN* (75 and 76), whereas it does not occur at all in *CT*. This is in itself one of the (Church's) 'signs of the times' and is concerned with what Karl Barth would have called the sin of sloth and neglect.

4. THE CONFLICT MODEL

This model attempts to do more than simply reinterpret the contents of the Gospel and reinstitutionalise the Church in accordance with the Gospel. It aims to make members of the Church conscious, by means of critical reflection and closely allied critical praxis, of the latent tensions and conflicts that fetter the meaning and value-systems of the Church and the Church itself and to break those chains so that the Church can be reformed and built up again and Christian faith can be improved in every way.

These tensions and conflicts are very varied. They occur within the Church and also have a bearing on the relationship between the Church and the world. They are financial and economic, juridical, political, social and ideological. They often originate with unjustified claims to power and interests. In that case, an important part is played in this model by the criticism of ideology, which enables the ideological legitimation of these claims to power and interests to be critically examined. Translating this into the language of faith, it is possible to say that catechesis conducted according to this model is directed towards the *ecclesia semper purificanda* and *metanoia*, which presupposes a continuous movement away from the sin of the established *status quo* of the Church.

What, then, is the position of *CT* with regard to a form of catechesis based on the conflict model and orientated towards an *ecclesia semper purificanda*? Following the teaching of Vatican II about the sinner in the Church (*Lumen gentium* 14), *CT* affirms that the Church consists of people who are sinful, but at the same time sanctified (29). The document does not, however, make the step from the sinner or sin in the Church to the sin of the Church, although that step would not be wrong, particularly in the context of catechesis as the Church's instrument of socialisation. Young people are, because of the psychological process of development that is taking place in them, especially alert to the discrepancy between the meaning and value-systems proclaimed by the Church on the one hand and the meaning and value-systems which the Church aims to achieve and in fact achieves on the other. There are ample examples of this discrepancy. To mention only a few, there is the discrepancy between the unity proclaimed by the Church and the divisions that really exist in the Church, that between the love proclaimed by the Church and the lack of love existing, for example, in the matter of divorce and homosexuality and finally that between the Church's call for peace and its factual defence of 'just war' or just deterrence. There is a strong tendency in this psychological process of development for the power of values to convince and gain recruits to diminish as the discrepancy between their proclamation and their factual existence increases. This can be expressed paradoxically in the following way: As the Church loses sight of its own (structural) sinfulness, young people especially lose their sense of the Church's holiness.

Another question also arises in this context. To whose advantage does the proclamation of these values take place and to whose disadvantage is silence maintained about the discrepancy between their proclamation and their factual existence? The question about *cui bono* and *cui malo* is, in this model, essential to catechesis. It is co-determinative for the future of the Church. Weber outlined very clearly the great importance of the problem of theodicy for the continued existence of religious institutions. Briefly summarised, the question posed by the theodicy is: How can the evil of injustice exist in the presence of a just God? This question penetrates to the very heart of our faith in creation and redemption and, in a society that is permeated with injustice, calls for clarification on the part of the Church, whose credibility and survival are directly involved in it. Yet there is no trace of this problem in *CT* and that is obviously wrong.

Have I perhaps been too negative in my assessment? It is unfortunately true that the conflict model is not discussed in *CT*, but liberation theology has a place in *EN*, a document to which *CT* often appeals, and it is implied in the latter in the concept of 'integral liberation' (29). With this liberation theology, *EN* clearly recognises oppressive social structures (36) and the Church's liberating task in that respect (30), liberating, what is more, on the basis of anthropological, theological and evangelical considerations (31). This brings us to the fifth model.

5. THE REVOLUTION MODEL

This model is widely used by historical materialists. It is orientated towards the educational preparation for the disappearance of bourgeois society and bourgeois institutions in that society—the State, the family, militarism and bourgeois morality. It is also directed towards the disappearance of the Church, in so far as it perpetuates bourgeois oppression and stands in the way of social liberation, which is the objective in the revolutionary struggle. That struggle is conducted in the light of a revolutionary morality, which does not recognise abstraction, absolute values, eternal values and metaphysical aspects, but is simply the rule of life of revolutionary action in solidarity. It is clear, then, that there could be no place in *CT* and *EN* for the revolutionary struggle against bourgeois society and the Church, which might legitimate that society and therefore contribute to oppression. It had certainly to be excluded as a possible aim of catechesis within the Church. This is not explicitly stated in *CT*, unless an explicit reference to *Rerum Novarum* and the social doctrine of the Church, which Ghenu demonstrated with great clarity to be bourgeois in character, points with sufficient plainness in that direction (29). In *EN*, however, the debate with liberation theology, which is assumed to be sympathetically disposed towards the revolutionary struggle, is extensively developed and conducted at a polemical level. Its theological legitimacy is disputed, its spirituality is exposed and its revolutionary and violent character, which it is presumed to possess, is mentioned at least three times and rejected (*EN* 37). Several questions arise in this context. What is the reason for this undifferentiated judgement or condemnation of liberation theology? Why was the existence of at least four tendencies within the sphere of liberation theology, displaying considerable variation in the use or rejection of Marxist analytical instruments and of revolutionary violence, not been taken into consideration in *EN*? And finally, *cui bono* and *cui malo*? To whose advantage and to whose disadvantage does this undifferentiated judgement take place?

6. CONCLUSIONS

The following conclusions can be drawn from this discussion of the five socialisation models and their application to *CT* and *EN*:

(**a**) The *incorporation model* occupies an important place in *CT* and it does not discount the tension between maintenance and change that is inherent in all intergenerative transference and the impossibility of total identification.

(**b**) The *adaptation model* occupies a central position together with the incorporation model in *CT*. It does not, however, take into consideration the social context in which the Church is placed and changes in this context.

(**c**) Unlike *EN*, *CT* is extremely cautious with regard to the *reform model*. It has a virtually defensive attitude. This means that there is not sufficient scope in *CT* for dialogue with other Christian churches and other religions. There is also insufficient scope for dialogue with secularisation. *EN* is much more open in this respect.

(**d**) The *conflict model* is implicitly rejected by *CT*. *EN* does not recognise variety in liberation theology or theologies. The result is that not only the conflict model, but also the revolutionary model are rejected by *EN*, the latter explicitly. This is regrettable.

(**e**) The *revolutionary model* is not discussed in *CT*. This is understandable, since it had already been explicitly rejected by *EN*, to which *CT* refers.

7. FINAL COMMENTS

Attitudes towards the process of socialisation and activities connected with it in the Church that place a one-sided emphasis on the two extremes in the continuum, in other words, on the incorporation and the revolution models, are bound to be disastrous for the future of the Church. The tension between maintenance and change is lost in these two models—change is lost in the incorporation model and maintenance is lost in the revolution model. The future of the Church, seen as an intergenerative problem, is furthered by attitudes towards socialisation and activities connected with it that are derived from the area in between the two extremes. In other words, more attention should be given to the reform and the conflict models and a more positive assessment of them should be made than is the case in *EN* and even more conspicuously in *CT*. If this is not done, there will be less likelihood in the long run that we shall be able to give a positive answer to the question: Does the Church still have a future?

Translated by David Smith

Bibliography

P. Berger *Heretical Imperative* (New York 1979); L. Boff *Die Kirche als Sakrament im Horizont der Welterfahrung* (Paderborn 1972); A. Camps *Partners in Dialogue. Christianity and Other World Religions* (New York 1983); M.-D. Chenu *La 'Doctrine sociale' de l'église comme idéologie* (Paris 1979); N. Elias *Über den Prozess der Zivilisation* (Berne 1969); A. Felling, J. Peters and O. Schreuder 'Identitätswandel in den Niederlanden' *Kölner Zeitschrift für Soziologie und Sozialpsychologie* 34 (1982) 26–53; J. Habermas *Theorie des kommunikativen Handelns I–II* (Frankfurt 1982); F. X. Kaufmann *Kirche begreifen* (Freiburg 1979); H. Kreutz *Soziologie der Jugend* (Munich 1974); J. B. Metz *Faith in History and Society* (London 1980); J. Moltmann *The Church in the Power of the Spirit* (London 1977); E. Schillebeeckx *Christ. The Christian Experience in the Modern World* (London 1980) *Christ. The Experience of Jesus as Lord* (New York 1980); H. R. Schlette *Glaube und Distanz* (Düsseldorf 1981); *Sozialisation, Identitätsfindung, Glaubenserfahrung* ed. G. Stachel (Zürich 1979); M. Weber *Gesammelte Aufsätze zur Religionssoziologie* (Tübingen 1922).

Gottfried Bitter

What Faith Shall We Hand On? Can It Be Reduced to Kerygmatic Essentials?

1. A THRONG OF QUESTIONS ARISES

PEOPLE GENERALLY begin to ask what the essentials of the Christian faith are at times when the Christian ship is having a rough passage, and only seems to have two courses open to it: to keep afloat with a minimum cargo, or to run aground in the full pomp of all the treasures it has on board. There is a widespread impression that religion has become remote from society in general;[1] and this would seem to justify the metaphor about the endangered cargo 'transmission of the faith'. Everyday life in our rationalising societies is automated and media-dominated, yet the dream-world of many people is shot through with the nightmare images of a nuclear catastrophe and a poisoned planet. This remarkable intertwining of a routine and practised harmony with unbridled apocalyptic paralyses the expression of Christian confidence and is an irritant preventing it from being heard. In this situation only comparatively few people associate real hope with the faith of Christians; most people are simply not interested in the Christian proclamation. The Christian ship is undoubtedly having a difficult passage. This state of affairs *compels* us to ask: What message does faith really have? What can it mean for men and women today, people who are living, working, caught up in relationships, bearing responsibility, searching for significance and identity, are anxious about peace and troubled about our environment? What can it say to people who are supposed to be able to live tomorrow in a future which is still largely shrouded in darkness?

We can of course direct our gaze, not towards the life of men and women, but directly towards the survival of Christians and churches. Then the question would be given a different stress. We should then have to ask: What form does the process of transmitting faith have to take if there are still to be Christians and churches the day after tomorrow? What social and cultural conditions determine the future handing on of the Christian faith?[2] Or we may redirect the question more firmly towards the content of what is to be transmitted and ask: In passing on the faith, what absolutely has to find expression, if yesterday's Christians are still to be able to recognise the faith of Christians tomorrow as their own? What *must* be said if faith is to keep its identity?

Whatever criteria we choose in defining the essentials, a conception about the total volume of the cargo of tradition is also required. But is there any such thing as a collective stock from which we can then make a selection, according to particular aspects? The idea goes against the grain. Faith is not an agglomerate of truths; nor is it a jumble of truths differing in their importance. But what has to be reduced or concentrated, if not a whole that can be given some contours or other?

2. THREE CAUTIOUS, FORMAL ANSWERS

But enough of questions. In discussing them, and others like them, people concerned with religious education have arrived at three insights which today may be said to meet with general agreement.

(a) In the religious instruction that takes its bearings from neo-scholasticism, faith is a sum of doctrinal tenets which have been passed down and have to be believed. If this is to be capable of existential assimilation, it has to be concentrated. Credit for this recognition goes to the movement towards kerygmatic renewal. 'The demand that in our proclamation it is primarily the kerygma which must come to the fore is directed, not merely against the simple adding together of continually new, individual pieces of knowledge and forms of piety. It is also levelled against any excessive breakdown of the substance of faith in the proclamation, and against a proliferation of tenets of merely peripheral importance.'[3] The existential *in*tensity with which faith is personally adopted can only be increased at the cost of the *ex*tension of the subject-matter of the faith that is passed on.

(b) The necessary reduction of the tenets of faith to be passed on cannot be determined merely in the light of the theological 'hierarchy of truths'. What appears in boldface type in dogmatics does not always coincide with what makes most impact on people of a particular age, belonging to a particular social and cultural environment, and with a particular intellectual background; it is not necessarily the things that give Christians joy in their faith, or which let them live in that faith. The 'existential hierarchy of truths'[4] is not necessarily congruent with the theological hierarchy of truths. Both have to be taken into account when faith is handed on. What we communicate to people who are involved in the process of learning to believe must be subjected to two questions: Does it represent the message of faith as a whole? and: Is it relevant for a particular group of people?[5]

(c) A selection of articles of faith, however justifed and however well chosen, can never illuminate more than *some aspect* of faith. Thus the 'content' of faith compared with its structural aspect is overstressed—its character as potential for solving human questions and problems, as against its own questionable and problematical aspects; its form as text, as against its practical character; its closedness as answer, as against its openness as a complex of experience. Over against this it is important to remind people that the foundation of faith is itself experience; to bring to mind the venture inherent in faith; to bring out the courage inspired by hope which we find in Abraham, Jesus and the apostles; and to show the structural comparability between the situation of believers yesterday and their situation today. 'The interpretation of faith which has been passed down to us did not descend from heaven at some point or other, finished and complete. It was worked out, prayed for, suffered. It is the testimony of shared experiences of faith and the expression of historically moulded answers to historically moulded questions.'[6] Finally, we must counter the timid desire to preserve what has been passed down, by talking about the living Spirit of God who continually reveals himself anew, keeps the history of faith and our own personal histories from becoming stagnant, and also calls us to see what has been transmitted to us in a new light.

All in all, if we want to make clear faith's life-determining power, we must concentrate its message and reduce it to its essentials.[7] This concentration should take account of both the theological *and* the existential hierarchy of truths, and will ideally mean the inspiration to live differently. But this will result not so much from a skilful selection of tenets of faith as from making their control 'flow' more. Faith will only be infectious if, instead of presenting itself to today's experience as the eternal truth of yesterday, it works out to an equal degree the experiential ground of faith and the claim to truth of these experiences.[8]

We shall become alive to the form in which Christian faith is most likely to make people prick up their ears once we examine our everyday experiences for the pattern of interpretation which is their implicit foundation, when we try to detect without any illusion what really impels us in this or that field of action, when we take seriously the trivial techniques we use to establish our own identity, since this essentially contributes to our personal survival—in short, when we become sensitive to the diverse forms of 'believing' which apply to people in a particular social context. Insight into the *de facto* hierarchy of truths shaped by the everyday world points the way to a recognition of the possible (existential) hierarchy of faith's truths which is of such importance in religious instruction. The answer to the question: What faith should we hand on? depends essentially on what 'faith' the addressee of the proclamation brings with him.

Liberation from the enslavement of the law means something different for a 20-year-old English punk from what it means for the aged Italian cardinal of the Roman curia. If the message of faith is to be 'address', the proclamation must be able to express itself in the language of the people with whom it has to do in any given case; and it must see this as a challenge of a particular kind. A general answer to the question of what is most necessary must therefore inevitably be initially a formal one; it can merely try to name criteria which should be taken into account in each given case when the message of faith is condensed. For 'what "belongs" to Christian identity—what essentially defines that identity—has to be newly "discovered" in each case in the unique and undeducible historical situation'.[9]

3. FOUR SUBSTANTIAL RECOMMENDATIONS

Without watering down these theological and didactic arguments for a deliberate restriction to formal criteria in passing on faith today and tomorrow, there are still certain Christian convictions and attitudes which have supported the lives of Christians yesterday and today, and which will support the life of men and women tomorrow in a way that still has to be realised.

(*a*) Life lived in the spirit of the Christian faith will be an alert life, a life open to the world. Christians will be living in a radically diaspora situation, in the midst of a world no longer shaped by Christian values. This will only allow Christian forms of living and the convictions of faith to be successfully transmitted by way of a critically productive discussion with the different worlds surrounding them. Vatican II valiantly led the way in this open-minded way of handing on faith[10] and the post-conciliar texts open up important new ways through the thickets.[11] The pictures and metaphors about the leaven and the grain of mustard seed, the people of God and God's vineyard all indicate that the goodness of God takes form only in the closest of human societies; and the kingdom of God grows only in the critical ferment[12] of societies and cultures. The courage for this open discussion takes its impetus from the Easter optimism that the God of Abraham and the God of Jesus Christ has always wished and worked for the success of human life in history. Christians call upon themselves and other people to co-operate in this dramatic process. The assent to the convicton that 'God wills and gives effect to our lives in this history' is what they call faith. In the discovery and venture of this faith the Christian is able to accept himself and his world: he finds himself to be someone who is sought out, wanted and loved.[13] By exposing themselves to this world, Christians lay themselves open on this world's behalf to the God in whom they believe. The purpose of handing on a faith reduced to its kerygmatic essentials will be to pass on these discoveries of faith today and tomorrow.

(*b*) A handing on of the faith that expresses a life springing from the experiences of faith—experiences not infrequently expressed through the prayer of complaint[14]—this will then lead people to the most important witness to God's love for human beings: Jesus, the messiah whom God both forsook and exalted. For the incomparably unique assurance of God and the 'incomparably attentive commitment to the poor mutually condition and explain one another in Jesus' special humanity and mortal nature, which is the place where the God who is creative love is revealed and experienced. God is manifested as the Father of Jesus Christ, and Jesus is manifested as the Son of the Father. To acquire a share in this relationship of Jesus' to God is the very definition of the wonder and mystery of the Christian faith'.[15]

If Jesus thus emerges as the Christ of both God and human beings, then the perilous operation which God set on foot in order to make human history succeed emerges too: the wisdom of God found in the scandal of the cross (1 Cor. 1:23ff.; Gal. 3:13). For Jesus' life and death reveal the living power and the deadly seriousness of God's love for men and women: God empties himself on the cross in the emptying of his witness—'for us' (Phil. 2:5–11; Rom. 5:15; 2 Cor. 5:21). The raising of Jesus is the verification of Jesus' life and death as God's epiphany, and at the same time the judgment on 'the wisdom of the wise and the cleverness of the clever' (1 Cor. 1:19). That is why every Christian proclamation will follow Paul's well-proved resolve 'to know nothing except Jesus Christ and him crucified' (1 Cor. 2:2). Anything that may be said about redeemed, saved and whole life will point to the cross of Jesus Christ as the fundamental structure of the new life and the new world.

(*c*) If the life and faith of Christians as the trusting acceptance of the divine loving kindness which is now taking on power (see Titus 3:4) is passed on by deed and word, then the communication of faith will take the form of an invitation to life.[16] Anyone who looks at the ministry of Jesus as this is passed down by the gospels comes upon different processes: proclamation and instruction, challenge and profession of faith; but at the centre of all these is always the invitation.[17] Invitation seems to be the ground base of Jesus' ministry. He proclaims the invitation of God as 'gospel' (Mark 1:1,15). For Zacchaeus and the Samaritan woman he shows himself to be the invitation of God in person (see Luke 19:1–10; John 4:7–26) and he promises God's universal, perfect and absolute invitation (Luke 14:15–24; see Isa. 25.6ff.; Rev. 7:17). What is being offered is 'abundance of life' (John 10:10); that is obvious from the chosen image of the banquet. The eucharist in the community of his people recalls this invitation, makes it present and anticipates it.

(*d*) These essential themes of the Christian faith we have to hand on can lead to a soteriological concentration[18] which then, entirely as a matter of course, opens out into doxology. For this is talk about people who, in the midst of their histories of hope and anxiety, and in their experience of guilt and forgiveness, find themselves overtaken by the dynamic force of the love of God in which they believe. Because their exodus progress with the God of Abraham and Jesus Christ finds expression, this same God is given the glory, since the well-being of human beings *is* God's glory;[19] because this proclamation of faith leads people to Jesus Christ as the One crucified and raised, hope for the future of God and human beings is strengthened; because the Church in its individual congregations is experienced as a fellowship of hope, it becomes the sign of God's quite specific invitation; because Christians now really hope for the growth of 'the new earth', they glorify the power of the Holy Spirit in our history. In this way liturgy and catechesis, martyrdom and the service, instruction and celebration, begin to converge.

Finally, we ought probably to ask: How can Christians and the Church be bold enough today to talk about the real possibilities of handing on the faith we have described tomorrow and the day after? When we remember the history of the life and faith of Christians and churches, are we not bound to reject any such prospect as either utopian or cynical? Are Christians so blind that they cannot see the miserable condition they are in today—a condition which they have also brought on themselves? Isn't the sum total of the failure of Christian proclamation and instruction so overwhelming that we should do better to desist from any further 'perversions of God' for the future?

It ill becomes Christians or churches to pass judgment on the Christian faith and living of past generations. But if they hear the call to repentance today and turn to a new life in the spirit of Jesus, they are then desiring to choose life in this God (see Amos 5:4), and are thereby showing their confidence that the God of Jesus Christ is a power in history which changes life and the world, and which will not be held back, either by our gods (see Isa. 41:21–29) or by our sins (see Isa. 1:18ff.). Where this confidence grows, it will be a matter of course to ask: How can we hand on to the coming generation the best thing in our lives? How can we prepare the way for God's coming for the next generation?[19] In these questions the answers we have found about the reduction to kerygmatic essentials may perhaps be important, as an expression of faith's assurance that in human history God is and will be the Lord and the perfecter, for our benefit and for his glory. 'For our salvation depends on hope' (Rom. 8:24).

Translated by Margaret Kohl

Notes

1. See most recently *Concilium* 165 (1983): *Indifference to Religion*; N. Mette *Voraussetzungen christlicher Elementarerziehung* (Düsseldorf 1983) pp. 29–56.
2. See F.-X. Kaufmann *Kirche begreifen* (Freiburg 1979) esp. pp. 147–187; R. Preul *Religion— Bildung—Sozialisation* (Gütersloh 1980) esp. pp. 143–270.
3. J. A. Jungmann *Glaubensverkündigung im Lichte der Frohbotschaft* (Innsbruck 1963) pp. 60f.
4. See K. Rahner 'Hierarchie der Wahrheiten' *Diakonia* 13 (1982) 376–382.
5. On this complex, see the discussion about a didactic of correlation which has been intensively pursued in German studies on religious education since about the middle of the 70s: G. Fuchs 'Glaubenserfahrung—Theologie—Religionsunterricht. Ein Versuch ihrer Zuordnung', K.Bl.103 (1978) 190–216; G. Baudler *Religiöse Erziehung heute* (Paderborn 1979); G. Bitter 'Was ist Korrelation? Versuch einer Bestimmung' K.Bl.106 (1981) 343ff.
6. *Zielfelderplan für den katholischen Religionsunterricht in der Grundschule*, Pt. I (*Grundlegung*) (Munich 1977) p. 17.
7. See especially K. E. Nipkow 'Das Problem der Elementarisierung der Inhalte des Religionsunterrichts' in *Lehrplanarbeit im Prozess* ed. G. Biemer and D. Knab (Freiburg 1982) pp. 73–95; also his *Grundfragen der Religionspädagogik*, III (Gütersloh 1982) pp. 191–222.
8. I am indebted to Rudolf Englert for the description of these three formal answers, which he provided in the course of discussion.
9. J. Werbick *Glaube im Kontext, Prolegomena zu einer elementaren Theologie* (Zürich 1983) p. 40.
10. See especially the constitutions *Lumen gentium* and *Gaudium et spes*, the decree *Ad gentes* and the declaration *Dignitatis humanae*.

11. As well as the important encyclicals *Populorum progressio* (1967) and *Evangelii nuntiandi* (1975) mention must be made of the apostolic letter *Catechesi tradendae* (1979)—especially Article 53—and the final document of the Third General Assembly of the Latin American episcopacy in Puebla (1978), particularly Articles 384–443.

12. Note here the use of the word 'transformare' in Article 17ff. in the encyclical *Evangelii nuntiandi*: AAS 68 (1976) 5–76.

13. For more detail see G. Fuchs 'Roter Faden Theologie—eine Skizze zur Orientierung' K.Bl.107 (1982) 165–180.

14. For more detail see O. Fuchs *Die Klage als Gebet. Eine theologische Besinnung am Beispiel des Psalms 22* (Munich 1982) esp. pp. 354–359.

15. See G. Fuchs, the article cited in note 13, 171.

16. See G. Bitter ' "Kommt und seht", Überlegungen zu einem einladenden Religionsunterricht' in *Religionsunterricht und Schülerpastoral* ed. A. Biesinger and W. Neuhoff (Munich 1982) pp. 13–32.

17. See A. Grabner-Haider *Verkündigung als Einladung* (Mainz 1968).

18. In this way a concentration can take the place of a dangerous reduction of the convictions of faith; see note 3 above. In the background is the far-reaching debate about the abbreviated formulas of faith. This was set on foot by K. Rahner in 'The Need for a "Short Formula" of Christian Faith' in *Theological Investigations*, IX, (London 1972) p. 117ff.; and see *ibid.*, XI, p. 230ff. It was pursued further by the following: R. Bleistein *Kurzformeln des Glaubens, Prinzip einer modernen Religionspädagogik* (Würzburg 1971); A. Stock *Kurzformeln des Glaubens, Zur Unterscheidung des Christlichen bei K. Rahner* (Einsiedeln 1971); W. Beinert 'Kurzformeln des Glaubens—Reduktion oder Konzentration?' in Th.PQ.122 (1974) 105–117; *Den Glauben bekennen—Formel oder Leben?* ed. G. Baudler, W. Beinert and H. Kretzer, (Würzburg 1975).

19. See the working paper of the Würzburg Synod 'Das katechetische Wirken der Kirche' in *Gemeinsame Synode der Bistümer in der Bundesrepublik Deutschland*, II ed. L. Bertsch *et al.* (Freiburg 1977). On the whole subject, see A. Exeler *et al.*, *Grundriss des Glaubens, Katholischer Katechismus* (Munich 1980).

PART III

Perspectives

James Fowler

A Gradual Introduction into the Faith

TRADITIONAL CATHOLIC scholastic theology observed a useful distinction between two different ways of understanding faith. 'The Faith', as used in the title I was assigned for this article, the scholastics referred to as 'fides quae creditur'—the 'faith *which is* believed'. They spoke of the activity, the way of being that is faith, with the phrase 'fides qua creditur'—the 'faith *by which (it) is* believed'.[1] This traditional and familiar distinction proves useful in addressing my assigned topic, 'The Gradual Introduction into the Faith', for in order to be faithful to the dynamics of the appropriation and transformation of faith we must clarify both the substance of faith—the contents of the Christian story and vision—and the dynamic activity by which it develops as a vital and animating centring in the lives of persons.

In this brief article I will attempt a trialectic. I will begin by characterising the narrative structure of the Christian story—the 'fides quae creditur'. Next, drawing on ten years of research and writing. I will address the question of the dynamics of persons' appropriation of the transformation by the Christian faith—the 'fides qua creditur'. And then, in a closing section, I will point to some principles that might guide our intentional efforts toward creating the contexts by which the Spirit of God can bring the human activity of faith into transforming and redeeming interplay with the Christian story.[2]

1. THE FAITH WHICH IS BELIEVED—THE CHRISTIAN STORY

Certainly one of the striking features of twentieth century thought at every level is its appropriation of 'process' as a fundamental or root metaphor for interpreting and managing our experiences. At every systems level and in every discipline dynamism and process are king, and substance, stasis, and immutability have been de-throned. One of the reasons for the growing interest in theology as 'story' and in explorations of the return to narrative as the primary mode of theological work, has to do with the dynamic character of narrative, as opposed to ontological categories inherited from pre-processial metaphysical perspectives. But the turn to narrative grows out of another critical reaction, this time to processial thought itself. The language and imagery of process has, itself, taken on highly abstract and formal modes of expression.[3] The turn to narrative, therefore, reflects a deepgoing need to reunite process with particular contents and contexts. It reflects a hunger to recover a sense of meanings as connected with history, of disclosure and depth as connected with experience.

47

Alasdaire MacIntyre's seminal book, *After Virtue*,[4] helps us see the critical and constructive role of narrative in the development of a *paideia*[5]—an approach to the intentional formation of persons of virtue and strength in any community. MacIntyre contends that virtues, understood as moral strengths and habits, are defined and valued in relation to the particular 'social *praxis*' of a given community or culture. The social praxis means, literally, the accepted and customary ways things are done in a society, and the meanings attached to them. A given social praxis is legitimated and sacralised, MacIntyre suggests, by the shared mytho-poetic 'narrative structure' which gathers and grounds the world-views, the beliefs, and the values of a people and culture.

Our concern with narrative and with *paideia* ('a gradual introduction into the faith') leads us to ask: What *is* the narrative structure of the Christian faith? What are the constituent elements of the Christian story and vision? If we had to accept the challenge recalled in the ancient Rabbinnic story, in which a young candidate for the Rabbinate was required to tell the meaning of the Law and the Prophets while standing on one foot, how might we draw its outlines?

Our response to this question here must be kept to the barest of outlines. My account of the narrative structure of the Christian master story,[6] however, would point to seven chapters: (1) GOD. 'In the beginning was the Word (Logos), and the Word was with God and the Word was God. . . .' In the Christian master story we cannot get behind this beginning point. The principle of Being is Being-Itself.[7] 'In the beginning, God . . .' (2) CREATION. In the dynamic expression of being God gives being. *Ex nihilo*, out and from nothing, from and by the Word, being is differentiated, separated in its unity and seeds of freedom and generative loci of Logos are dispersed. The inner life of God makes room for participation. (3) FALL. Finite freedom and vulnerability and the seeds of freedom grow into the illusion (and burden) of self-groundedness. Cleaved loci of Logos undertake to be primally creative, rather than participative. This results in breach, alienation, and enmity, between God and God's creation, and between the created. (4) COVENANT. God makes initiatives of reconciliation; God offers liberation (from bondage, from self-groundedness) and the invitation to reconciled partnership. God gives the gift, the grace, of *Way* (Torah, Law). Then the narrative shows us a series of oscillations between covenant-falling away, covenant-falling away, covenant-falling away, until (5) INCARNATION. Logos enfleshed. God discloses in human being the erotic intention in creation and its intended culmination in a unity of rich and variegated harmony. The intended already-but-not-yet character of the universal commonwealth of love is foretold and instantiated in word, deed, death and resurrection. The CROSS shows in double disclosure the depth of divine love and the pattern of the evil structures and resistance of human enmity toward God's future. (6) Resurrection and Spirit confirm and empower CHURCH in its calling to partnership with the risen Christ in reconciling, healing, and the incarnational proclamation of the inbreaking commonwealth of love. (7) Finally, continually coming to us, and to all presents and pasts, from the Sovereign Power of the Future, the lure and imperative of the commonwealth of love exerts its ultimately undefeatable power for newness, justice and liberation-redemption. In the energy-field released in the spirit of the risen Christ, and lured by the already-but-not-yet power of the commonwealth of love, we are called to be in and to call others to the vocation of partnership with God. This calling, this vocation, is the secret entrusted to faith; a secret we are mandated to disclose and proclaim in the power of the Spirit.

2. THE FAITH BY WHICH IT IS BELIEVED—A DEVELOPMENTAL VIEW

The elements of the Christian story and vision sketched in the previous section will be drawn differently by various theologians and theological communities of the Church. The narrative structure, however, will not depart very far from the kind of chapters suggested here. This claim rests upon the integrity and structure of the Christian story. This brings us to the question that centrally concerns Christian *paideia*: How do we dependably and faithfully facilitate a formative and reformative developmental dialectic between the Christian story and the stories-in-process of contemporary persons and groups? How do we as educators and communities of formation provide for the 'gradual introduction into the faith'?

When the scholastics recognized the need to address the 'fides qua creditur'—the faith by which (it) is believed—they acknowledged the crucial importance of what they would have called the 'subjective' aspect of faith. For them, the *fides quae* . . . could be taken as a *depositum*, a firmly fixed, objective foundation of revealed truth. Historical critical method in the studies of scripture and tradition have given us much more dynamic understandings of the evolution of sacred texts, and of the intermixing of event and mythos in the construction of the Christian master story. Its objectivity—what I called its structure and integrity—are grounded in different understandings of truth and Logos than were held by the scholastics. Similarly, understandings of the person appropriating 'the faith' have changed. Process notions, centered in the metaphor of 'development', have pervasively affected our ways of understanding our own lives and experience, and of trying to provide for the formation and ongoing growth of persons in faith.

Among the developmental perspectives on human growth and change, I and my associates have undertaken to study what has come to be called 'faith development'. While detailed discussion of our research and theory will have to be pursued elsewhere,[8] here a few of our findings can be sketched.

We began our research with the premiss that faith is a human universal. By this we mean that wherever we find human beings, our species is marked by the awareness of death, by the facing of limits, by the burdens of choice under conditions of uncertainty, and by struggle with the questions of destiny and ultimate meaning. Usually these issues of faith, in our collective history, have been addressed through the mediation of religion—the collective expression through rite, myth, symbol, ethical teachings and music, of human apprehensions of, and by, transcending truth. In the modern period, however, marked by pluralism, secularism, and the anomic breakdown of communal grounding in shared master stories, we have had to recognise that the activity of being and becoming in faith may take forms and struggle for integrity in directions other than through cultic or institutional religion. Hence, we may say that there are secular forms and objects of faith. There are stances toward the limiting conditions of human life which resemble religious faith in their functions, but which are more idiosyncratic, if not to say solipsistic.

Acknowledging these considerations, we have conducted research, via indepth semi-clinical interviews, with something approaching 500 persons over the last ten years. Among other goals, we have sought to *test whether certain developmental patterns which seem to hold in the domains of cognitive, psychosocial and moral growth have developmental parallels in the area of faith*. For purposes of this research we have employed a formal definition of faith. In its formality (its lack of specifying doctrinal or ethical content) we have hoped to gain access to secular and quasi-religious patterns of faith, as well as those which might be more accurately described as religious faith. Faith, we have said,[9] is:

People's evolved and evolving ways of experiencing self, others and world (as they construct them) as related to and affected by the ultimate conditions of existence (as they construct them) and of shaping their lives' purposes and meanings, trusts and loyalties, in light of the character of being, value and power determining the ultimate conditions of existence (as grasped in their operative images—conscious and unconscious—of them).

In the analysis of our data we have found suggestive grounds for proposing a sequence of stages to describe a general pattern of development in faith. These stages characterise a succession of styles of knowing and valuing, a succession of typical patterns of construal and commitment, which describe how persons periodically rework their ways of being in faith.[10] In briefest form the stages can be sketched as follows:

PRIMAL FAITH (Infancy): A pre-language disposition of trust forms in the mutuality of one's relationships with parents and others to offset the anxiety that results from separations which occur during infancy.

INTUITIVE-PROJECTIVE FAITH (Early childhood): Imagination, stimulated by stories, gestures, and symbols, and not yet controlled by logical thinking, combines with perception and feelings to create long-lasting images that represent both the protective and threatening powers surrounding one's life.

MYTHIC-LITERAL FAITH (Childhood and beyond): The developing ability to think logically helps one order the world with categories of causality, space, and time; to enter into the perspectives of others; and to capture life meaning in stories.

SYNTHETIC-CONVENTIONAL FAITH (Adolescence and beyond): New cognitive abilities make mutual perspective-taking possible and require one to integrate diverse self-images into a coherent identity. A personal and largely unreflective synthesis of beliefs and values evolves to support identity and to unite one in emotional solidarity with others.

INDIVIDUATIVE-REFLECTIVE FAITH (Young adulthood and beyond): Critical reflection upon one's beliefs and values, understanding of the self and others as part of a social system, and the assumption of responsibility for making choices of ideology and lifestyle open the way for commitments in relationships and vocation.

CONJUNCTIVE FAITH (Mid-life and beyond): The embrace of polarities in one's life, an alertness to paradox, and the need for multiple interpretations of reality mark this stage. Symbol and story, metaphor and myth (from one's own traditions and others'), are newly appreciated as vehicles for grasping truth.

UNIVERSALIZING FAITH (Mid-life or beyond): Beyond paradox and polarities, persons in this stage are grounded in a oneness with the power of being. Their visions and commitments free them for a passionate yet detached spending of the self in love, devoted to overcoming division, oppression, and brutality, and in effective anticipatory response to the inbreaking commonwealth of love.[11]

Regarding this description of stages several crucial clarifications must be kept in mind: Transitional phases, times for the relinquishing of one stage's way of making meaning and beginning the construction of a new one, come with experiences of dislocation and dissonance. Revelatory moments in a person's or group's life produce dissonance, as do the predictable and unpredictable disruptions due to maturation, change, or loss. The transitional phases are as important to care for in *paideia* as are the periods of growth within the equilibrium of a stage. In fact, in a Christian *paideia*—the 'gradual introduction into the faith'—careful provision needs to be made for anticipating and to some degree precipitating the transitions. Further, remember that this sequence of stages and transitions deal with emotional, volitional and cognitive development. Through the interaction of persons with the events and contexts of their lives, and with the store of images and meanings their communities offer, they form and reform convictional orientations that ground their characters and guide their actions and reactions. These stages describe, in formal, structural terms, the *patterns* of emotion-knowing that characterise our developmental movements as selves in community.[12] Moreover, the sequence of stages should be thought of as a widening spiral movement. Each new stage builds upon the strengths of previous ones, and carries forwards the emotion-knowing repertoires of earlier stages, while adding new strengths and comprehensiveness. There is, then, a kind of cumulative richness to the process of faith development. Finally, though each new stage adds dimensions of richness and comprehensiveness, it would be a mistake to equate development to any particular stage as *a'priori* necessary for salvation, or for giving a person or group worth. It seems likely that each successive stage also adds qualitatively new dangers in terms of capacities for self-deception and evil,[13] therefore increasing the need for vigilance and self-scrutiny before God, and for ongoing fidelity in binding the heart to holiness.

3. STAGES AND STORY: NOTES TOWARD A CHRISTIAN PAIDEIA

Many of our best efforts and designs in Christian catechesis in the United States are fundamentally self-defeating. Despite our attention to developmental theories, and our efforts to address people in developmentally appropriate ways, our intended dialectic between persons' lives and experiences and the Christian story often do not prove to set them on paths of radical trust and faithfulness. A principal set of reasons for this failure, I have come to believe, derives from our failure to recognise that Christian *paideia* means formation into an alternative consciousness. Christian *paideia* is formation for life as part of an intentional moral and faith minority. Grounded in the Christian story and vision, Christian *paideia* engenders a specific pattern of *virtues*, evokes a determinate cluster of life-shaping *emotions* (affections), calls us to a clear concept of *vocation* as partnership with God, and forms a community of sustaining, transforming *hope*. Its efforts will be diluted and ineffective if care is not taken to anticipate and counter the infectious images and values of self-groundedness celebrated by the larger culture. Yet, at the same time, a Christian *paideia* which frankly recognises the pluralism of our era, and takes Christian presence as a 'Public Faith'[14] seriously, will not call for or settle for a merely sectarian stance of the 'withdrawing' sort.[15] It envisions the nurturing of Christians who will become deeply and particularly identified with the Christian story and vision, but who will also develop the requisite levels of faith development to offer in a secular society—through their living and in a public language—the rich resources of the Christian tradition.[16]

The *virtues* engendered in Christian *paideia* begin with the 'great commandment'—the love of God, and love of neighbour. In a proper *paideia* radical self-love and the acids of an unhealthy narcissism would not be normative, either in persons or in community. Christian community and Christian families need to struggle toward a profound clarification of our socialisation of the very young. While egocentrism and self-assertion are an integral part of cognitive and emotional development, childrearing practices that avoid using competition and nefarious comparisons as methods of motivation can keep them from becoming normative. Similarly, parenting and patterns of socialisation into collective life that avoid making achievement and the exhibition of skills into conditions of worth can do a lot to mitigate the radical individualism of our common life. Moreover, familial and collective experiences of just community, where each person is treated with the regard due a child of God, and where correction and discipline are geared to reconciliation and responsible selfhood, engenders a 'taste' for justice, an awakening of moral imagination, and evokes the foundations of moral courage. The virtues deriving from love of God and neighbour formed in this kind of setting evolve toward justice and social righteousness, the forms which love of God and neighbour take in societal and world-societal terms.

There is a strong, though often neglected strand in the Christian tradition which holds that the heart of Christian *paideia* focuses on the forming of a distinct set of Christian emotions or affections. This approach takes on fresh dimensions as we learn more about the bi-hemispheric functioning of the human brain. In one recent presentation of this tradition, theologian Don Saliers identifies four clusters of specifically Christian emotions—deep dispositions shaping our persisting ways of moving into life. He speaks of (1) 'gratitude and giving thanks'; (2) 'holy fear and repentance'; (3) 'joy and suffering'; and (4) 'the love of God and the love of neighbour'.[17] This approach highlights liturgy and prayer as the contexts where the imagination and emotions are awakened and formed, and sees sacrament, image and music as indispensable elements in Christian *paideia*.

When asked, 'What does it mean to be a human being?' the Christian story answers; 'To respond affirmatively with your life to God's call to partnership.' Covenant and vocation, in response to the address of God, are the foundations of human ethical life, understood Christianly. Walter Brueggemann recently characterised vocation as 'Finding a purpose for one's life that is part of the purposes of God'.[18] The Christian story tells us that we are called to partnership in God's ongoing work of creation, governance and liberation-redemption. A significant part of Christian *paideia* involves helping persons find the linkages and imperatives by which their worldly work can be brought faithfully into participation in God's work.[19]

Christian *paideia* looks toward and draws upon a future which is not primarily defined by continuity with the past and the present. Informed by the vision and reality of the inbreaking-but-not-yet commonwealth of love, which is the promise and the gift of the Sovereign Lord of the Future, the Christian story calls us to be a community of profound hope. Not optimism, but hope. Such hope leads to an alternative reading of the signs of the times. It looks at the bleakness and danger of a world on the brink of nuclear disaster without either the inflation of total responsibility, or the despair of total helplessness. Trusting in a God who can cause the very stones to cry out when the prophets are silent, the Christian story leads us to hope and trust that God will not relinquish the role or the responsibility of Lordship of the Future, and that the fulfillment of a commonwealth of love will not be thwarted or defaulted.

Notes

1. Juan Alfaro 'II Faith' in *Encyclopedia of Theology: The Concise Sacramentum Mundi*. Karl Rahner (New York 1975) pp. 510–511.

2. For an account of the narrative structure of Christian Faith which I found suggestive as I worked out the next section, see Gabriel Fackre *The Christian Story: A Narrative Interpretation of Basic Christian Doctrine* (Grand Rapids, Michigan 1978)

3. Alfred North Whitehead *Process and Reality* (New York: 1929); John B. Cobb *A Christian Natural Theology* (Philadelphia, Pennsylvania, 1965); see especially John B. Cobb 'A Guide to the Literature', Appendix B of John B. Cobb, Jr. and David Ray Griffin *Process Theology: An Introductory Exposition* (Philadelphia, Pennsylvania 1976) pp. 162–185.

4. (Notre Dame, Indiana 1981).

5. The classical text on *Paideia* is that of Werner Jaeger, *Paideia: The Ideals of Greek Culture*. Three volumes. (Translated by Gilbert Highet). (New York, 2nd Edition, 1945). See also Jaeger's posthumously published *Early Christianity and Greek Paideia*. (London 1961).

6. For a development of the idea of a 'master story' see my *Stages of Faith: The Psychology of Human Development and the Quest for Meaning* (San Francisco 1981) pp. 277ff.

7. See Paul Tillich *Systematic Theology* I. (Chicago 1951).

8. *Stages of Faith: Life-maps: Conversations on the Journey of Faith* (With Sam Keen) (Waco, Texas 1978); see also 'Theology and Psychology in the Study of Faith Development' in 'The Challenge of Psychology to Faith' edited by Steven Kepnes and David Tracy. *Concilium* 156 (1982).

9. *Stages of Faith*, pp. 92–93.

10. Movement from one stage to another is not automatic or inevitable; persons can and do arrest or equilibrate in one or another of the stages. It is not uncommon to find adults who are best described by stages that have their rise in childhood or adolescence. For more adequate descriptions of this research and resulting findings, see *Stages of Faith*.

11. With only slight modifications this account of the stages is reprinted from 'Stages of Faith', a 'Psychology Today Conversation with James Fowler' in *Psychology Today*, 17, no. 11, (November 1983) 56–62.

12. Robert Kegan has written a book of great importance as regards understanding and working with transitions. Calling himself a 'neo-Piagetian', Kegan has begun to offer highly original and exciting extensions of the developmental perspective of Piaget into personality theory. *The Evolving Self* (Cambridge, Massachusetts 1982).

13. Herbert Fingarette *Self-Deception.* (London 1969); M. Scott Peck *People of the Lie: The Hope for Healing Human Evil* (New York 1938).

14. Martin E. Marty *The Public Church* (New York 1981); Parker J. Palmer *The Company of Strangers* (San Francisco 1982).

15. Ernst Troeltsch, in his monumental *The Social Teachings of the Christian Churches*, distinguishes between sect groups of the aggressive or social transforming type and those of the withdrawing type.

16. David Tracy's rich concept of the 'Christian classic' advances an important way of holding together the particularity and integrity of Christian commitment with the ability to speak from Christian convictions in genuinely public manner. See *The Analogical Imagination: Christian Theology and the Culture of Pluralism* (New York 1981).

17. Don Saliers *The Soul in Paraphrase* (New York 1980). See also Robert C. Roberts *Spirituality and Human Emotion* (Grand Rapids, Michigan 1982).

18. 'Covenanting as the Human Vocation' in *Interpretation* (1979) 126.

19. For a more extensive development of an image of Christian maturity as involving vocational partnership with the work of God, see my forthcoming *Becoming Adult, Becoming Christian* (San Francisco 1984).

Casiano Floristán

The Liturgy: the Place for Education in the Faith

THE COMING together of the liturgical and catechetical movements, along with the mutual influence of liturgical celebration and catechesis, has created a unique opportunity for enriching the Church's pastoral ministry. Today, the importance of the liturgy in the process of formation in the faith is obvious and equally evident is the contemporary desire to relate catechesis to the celebration of the liturgy as such.[1]

1. CHRISTIAN MYSTERY AND LITURGICAL ACTION

Throughout the course of its history, the *liturgical movement* has shown up the double polarity which exists between the liturgy's pastoral dimension and its specific use in sacred worship, between catechesis and what is essentially sacred and between faith and religion.[2] Time and again, the fact that the liturgy serves a dual purpose has been highlighted; its intrinsic two-way movement serves to worship God and to sanctify men (S.C. 10).[3] In any case, in contrast with a merely ceremonial or juridical understanding of Christian worship, the concept of liturgy has superseded its definition of being 'the public worship that the Church renders to God' and since Vatican II has been understood as 'the activity of the Church' (S.C. 10), 'the work of our redemption' (S.C. 2) or 'the proclamation of God's wonderful work in the history of salvation' (S.C. 35) which occurs within the missionary activity of the Church 'since the Church, in Christ, is in the nature of sacrament—a sign and instrument, that is, of communion with God and of unity among all men' (L.G. 1). Accordingly, it is no longer possible to understand the liturgy as an organisation of ritual which has no real relevance to life or to the experience of faith which precedes participation in the liturgy. In short, the liturgy consists of *mystery* and *action* and this means that it is a symbolic and effective action which makes the mystery of divine salvation present in those who believe.[4] This is why Pius X described the liturgy as 'the first and indispensable source of the real Christian spirit' and succeeding popes strongly encouraged the 'active participation' of the faithful in the celebration of the liturgy.[5]

At the very beginning of the liturgical movement, the value of the liturgy as a forum for instruction, especially in the pastoral field, was clearly emphasised. With the promulgation of the constitution *Sacrosanctum Concilium*, there was a shift of emphasis to the catechetical field. Finally, after the initial enthusiasm which immediately followed the

54

Council, areas of tension between 'evangelisers' and 'sacramentalists' began to emerge. At the beginning of the last decade, the binomial term 'evangelisation-sacramentalisation' began to be used at an official level. The administration of the sacraments takes into account the needs of large impersonal groups as well as those of the individual and can range from a truly spiritual experience to a merely magical formality; and in the light of this, there has been developing, sometimes even as a kind of protest, a form of evangelisation which attempts to arouse the faith of conversion from purely evangelical options and which also takes account of the historical contexts of our own age.[7] A new synthesis is therefore being achieved, though more so in the theological than in the pastoral field, by widening the understanding of the liturgy and the sacraments to include theological, anthropological and social contexts. From the point of departure of biblical and historical analysis, the understanding of the liturgy has followed the ups and downs of sacramental theology within the various religious, cultural, social and political contexts which essentially affect those who take part in the Christian assembly. Historically, the understanding of what a sacrament is has followed this line of development: 'a symbolic participation in the Christian mystery' (The Greek Fathers), 'a visible sign of invisible grace' (St Thomas), 'an instrument of grace' (Post-Tridentine Theology), 'a symbolic expression of the Church as sacrament' (Vatican II) and 'a sign of liberty and liberation' or 'a prophetic anticipation of the perfection on earth of the Kingdom of God' (Liberation Theology).[8]

2. FAITH AND THE LITURGY

The relationship between faith and the liturgy finds its roots in the patristic axiom 'legem credendi lex statuat supplicandi' which means that the prayer of the Church is the yardstick and standard or the expression of the faith.[9] However, the dogmatic implications of this quotation demand that its terms be properly defined: faith and prayer are united in symbol. So, just as any abuse of the liturgy can bring about a manipulation of the faith, dogmatic fossilisation can cause a distortion of the liturgy. Therefore, the statement of Pius XI that 'the liturgy is the principal organ of the *magisterium* of the Church'[10] has to be understood with some caution.

In any case, it can be affirmed that from the very beginnings of the Church, the faith and the liturgy have constituted a basic unity;[11] throughout the centuries, the relationship of one to the other has varied but in the liturgical reforms introduced by Vatican II it acquires a new and special emphasis. In the words of G. Lukken: 'The faith is much more than a condition for the liturgy, and the liturgy is more than a mere confirmation and ratification of the faith. It can be said that the faith is an integral part of the liturgy and, inversely, that the liturgy is an integral part of the faith'.[12] The faith is the basic criterion by which any expression of the sacred can be judged fit for use in Christian worship.[13]

3. THE LITURGY AND CATECHESIS

The relationship of the liturgy and catechesis to the Christian mystery varies according to the methods of practical application. Instruction in the faith which is the end and aim of catechesis, is closely linked to baptism, the sacrament of faith, and indeed to all the sacraments as professions of faith ('protestationes fidei'). St Ambrose stated; 'Fides tua pleno fulgeat sacramento'. The Constitution on the Liturgy declares that the sacraments 'not only presuppose faith, but by words and objects they also nourish, strengthen and express it' (S.C. 59). Precisely because the sacraments are *signs*, 'they also instruct' and so it is imperative to carry out a catechetical ministry, within and outwith the liturgy, so that 'the faithful may easily understand the sacramental signs' (S.C. 59).

Precisely because catechesis, then, derives as an intrinsic necessity from the liturgy, the latter, with its own specific character, is a form of practical catechesis. 'From its very beginnings, the Church has recognised that catechesis and the liturgy render each other mutual support'.[14] In this regard, both catechists and liturgists make similar statements. For instance, the liturgy is 'the teaching (*didaskalia*) of the Church' and 'permanent catechesis'[15] or 'complete instruction in the faith'.[16] In other words, 'the celebration of the liturgy is the specific place for education in the faith'.[17] A.-M. Triacca states that 'the liturgy celebrates the divine mysteries perpetuating them in the faith and through the faith. . . . Theology, on its own, is not conducive to salvation and neither is the faith, but when *the faith is celebrated*, sacred theology is lived out and Christian living attains its highest expression in liturgical celebration which is a profession and formulation of the faith, and in which the faith is put into practice, given public expression and made known'.[18]

The papal and episcopal *magisterium* expresses the relationship between catechesis and the liturgy in much the same way. 'Catechesis is intrinsically united to all liturgical and sacramental action'.[19] Again, the liturgy is 'an inexhaustible source of practical catechesis'.[20].

These foregoing theological statements have to be examined with care in the light of the reality of our liturgical celebrations. The Second General Conference of the South American Bishops, meeting in Medellín in 1968, states that 'the liturgy is not properly integrated into religious instruction if the mutual influence of both is not taken into account';[21] so that 'some previous catechetical instruction on the Christian mystery and its expression in the liturgy would always appear to be necessary'.[22] The difficulty of this task is evident because ten years later, the Third Conference, which met in Puebla in 1979, stated that 'it took account of the fact that there is a marked lack of catechetical instruction in the liturgy amongst the faithful'.[23]

It has been repeated frequently that the most effective form of catechetical instruction in the liturgy is the celebration of the liturgy itself. However, the difficulty of celebrating or taking part in a liturgical function which can both express the faith and also give instruction in it, is already well known.

Moreover, despite routine or lack of effort and preparation, etc., of the liturgy, it is only right that proper account should be taken of the historical role which the liturgy, as well as expressions of the sacred which rightly belong to popular Catholicism, has played over the centuries in keeping alive and in transmitting the faith. This transmission of the faith is particularly evident at those moments of history when the Church's activity has been almost exclusively reduced to worship alone. Of course, in this analysis, the intimate connection between the faith and its expression in divine worship cannot be ignored since the basic nucleus of all worship, especially amongst the ordinary people, is the religious phenomenon. In the secularised and disillusioned post-Christian world in which we live today, the liturgy has to face the ever increasing challenge of ceasing to be merely an expression of worship to become a genuine Christian celebration.[24]

4. CATECHETICAL PREREQUISITES FOR THE CELEBRATION OF THE LITURGY

(a) The liturgy must not be used as an instrument

Because of the fact that there are those who take part in divine worship without a personalised faith, whose commitment is immature and who possess only a superficial knowledge of the faith, there is always the obvious risk of using the liturgy as an *opportunity* for evangelisation and catechesis. It is hard to believe that when the liturgy is properly celebrated, it does evangelise those whose faith is in any way incomplete and it does catechise since we are all incipient catechumens till the end of our days.

Nowadays, it is almost unanimously recognised that since Christianity is, in itself, a symbolic entity, the process of evangelisation must contain a sacramental core if it is not to be reduced to a mere form of communicating yet another ideology. It is also being noted that the celebration of the liturgy is not simply an opportunity for evangelisation but is the very action of evangelising, carried out sacramentally. If the sacraments are signs of Jesus Christ, they must also be signs of our historical liberation or signs of Christ's work which, in turn, constitutes both the content and the task of evangelisation. In short, the good news which is proclaimed in evangelising is the very essence of what a sacrament is. In other words, the sacraments are signs of the same message or good news that evangelisation proclaims. The binomial term 'evangelisation-sacramentalisation' finds its origins in an understanding of the Church as a sacrament.[25]

(b) Finding a balance between the liturgies of the word and of the sacrament

The effect of the liturgical reforms in regard to the use of the vernacular, a biblical lectionary, a simplification of ritual and greater emphasis on historical contexts, has been to make a specially significant contribution to the liturgy of the word. The result of this is that its status has grown and it now takes up more time, it has also become more rational since it consists of words, and its possible uses have been increased to the extent that it is now employed on every possible occasion. The development of that part of the liturgy which is strictly sacramental has been reduced to a series of repetitive rites; variety has been curtailed by the limitation of the number of eucharistic prayers, there is hardly any opportunity for contemplation since the periods of silence are practically non-existent and symbolism has been reduced to the simplest forms with almost no opportunity for physical expression.[26]

While the complete liturgical celebration is and has to be an expression of faith, the catechetical nucleus of the liturgy of the eucharist consists of the confession of faith expressed in the biblical readings (proclamation), the creed (profession) and the eucharistic prayer (doxology). Singing, the use of symbols and periods of silence contribute towards the creation of an atmosphere conducive to the expression and fomenting of the faith which, in turn, is raised to God through prayer, whether it be of contrition, petition or thanksgiving.

Few adverse criticisms of the new lectionary can be made on catechetical grounds. There are occasions when the first reading at Sunday Mass is difficult to understand or to explain in a practical way. On some occasions, the second reading could easily serve as an introduction to the liturgy of the eucharist or as a conclusion to the whole liturgical celebration. The creed, previously sung and now recited, is excessively dogmatic as a profession of faith with too clearly defined an emphasis on ancient controversies. It ought to be an authentically communal profession of faith. Knowledge of the faith would be enriched by a greater variety of eucharistic prayers and there should be one for each major celebration of the eucharist throughout the liturgical year.

(c) The catechetical dimension of the homily should be emphasised

The homily is a liturgy in its own right and as such forms part of the complete celebration or the proclamation of the common faith. If this is taken into account, the homily can be given a catechetical slant by bearing in mind the following series of correlations; biblical interpretation—social application, preacher—listener, truth—

communication, religious language—the language of the people, and message—context.

Suitable material for any sermon is to be found in the gospels or in the good news of the kingdom of God. This message which is crystallised in the Scriptures, is also present in the depths of the human heart and in the sincerest desires of society at large.

Nevertheless, it is no easy task to make the Gospel relevant. The complexity of literary styles and the antiquity of the socio-cultural and economic realities of the Jewish people at the time of Our Lord make the preacher's task even more difficult. Exegesis must be a prerequisite of preaching but never its content and neither does the actual cultural context of that time in which Our Lord lived constitute material for a sermon.

Because in its essence the Christian faith has to be personalised, real human history forms a constitutive element of revelation. In other words, history must not be a *pre*text for preaching, nor must it be merely the *con*text in which preaching occurs but must form the *text* of that preaching since it is not possible for faith to begin or to mature except through personal and historical experience. In short, the subject matter chosen from the biblical readings has to be made relevant to a contemporary theme that affects the community. This is not always easy. At times, it will be possible to find a contemporary theme, but if the biblical texts have no direct bearing on any such theme it would be preferable, as an exception to the rule, to choose something more appropriate. Preaching must never be abstract.

Bearing in mind that every liturgical celebration is a form of preaching or of proclaiming the word of God, there is no reason why several people should not take part in the development of the homily. The possible forms that a homily can take cannot be limited to the alternatives of monologue or dialogue. Various forms can be found according to the way that different people are allowed to take part; one person could narrate the facts and this should normally be in the form of announcements, another could ask questions, someone else could make the Gospel message relevant and another could propose forms of commitment or of conversion.[27]

(d) The Christian assembly must form a minimal community

One inherited aspect of a clerical liturgy is that the major part is played by the priest celebrant almost to the exclusion of anyone else so that in most instances the role of the laity in liturgical celebrations is to be obedient, submissive and devout. It is still no easy task to get the laity to take an active interest in the liturgy and when lay people do try to participate, they are frequently frustrated.

The Vatican Council stressed that the subject of all liturgical celebrations is the assembled community of those who are baptised (one should also add evangelised and believing), but this principle is often neglected. As Congar puts it: the 'ecclesia' or Christian community is the integral subject of all liturgical action.[28]

Nevertheless, the ordinary subject of our liturgical celebrations, apart from exceptional circumstances, is the *family group* or the *socially mixed group*. The family is almost exclusively the subject of the four sacramental events of baptism, matrimony, the anointing of the sick and Christian burial; the family also plays an important part in the first communion of children, in ordination to the priesthood as well as in the sacrament of confirmation which is usually administered to large groups, which does not allow much opportunity for personal renewal. In short, apart from the eucharist and the sacrament of penance, the family (including the non-Christian one or the one whose faith is weak) has deprived the Christian assembly of its proper liturgical role. This displacement creates areas of dissatisfaction to the extent that it is increasingly difficult to restore to liturgical celebration a sense of the fact that it properly belongs to the people and to the Church Militant. It is my view that this serious problem will not be solved while the sacraments of Christian initiation are conferred on immature people, as has been the practice, with infant baptism, the reception of the eucharist in childhood, confirmation conferred during the immaturity of adolescence; and this even applies to Christian marriage which is frequently simply a form of civil marriage conducted by the Church. The trouble is that baptism, the sacrament of faith, which generates Christian life, only serves to mark the beginning of a vaguely religious life without any effective links with initiation as such and, consequently, becomes a subsequent cause of the decline of what is essentially sacramental.

Accordingly, liturgical instruction has to meet a daunting challenge. An adequate catechesis is not sufficient, albeit necessary. When the moment of conferring a sacrament arrives, any preceding catechesis will be totally ineffective if the liturgy is not properly celebrated. In any form of Christian initiation or re-initiation, the teaching of the faith must lead to a maturity of belief and more committed witness to the faith in the individual's life; it must also bring about a ratification of the faith by the profession of the faith both at the personal level and at the level of the group formed by the Christian assembly; otherwise, it is of little or no real value. The effort of making a journey can be satisfying in itself, but the mirage of setting off on a false pursuit can only lead to deception.

Moreover, parish masses are a clear example of a social coming together in which the faithful meet in physical proximity but without much mutual communication. In these circumstances, personal relationships do not exist and neither is there any opportunity for expressing the social or collective dimensions of the faith. At best, there is some bond of unity with the celebrating priest and, through him, with other parishes. But, as a general rule, a parish is not usually a community. It tends to be simply an association of a secondary nature and within its liturgical celebrations, there seems to be little opportunity for effective communication. The parish structure has been criticised, and with reason, for being exclusively a situation in which worship takes place and within which there is little room for prophetic activity and hardly any form of evangelisation. It is very often a situation in which *ceremonies* take place. However, despite that, it has to be rediscovered that the liturgy is of vital importance as a profession of faith, a cohesive source of unity, the point of departure for Christian commitment and the place for Christian celebration. To achieve these aims, it is imperative that a living Christian community should be built up within each parish.

(e) The cyclic nature of Christian instruction

Systematic instruction based on the Scriptures and on the liturgy functions in a cyclic form and revolves round a central core which is not an idea but an event. This fact is clearly discernible in the liturgical year. This annual repetition of festivals causes their celebration to become a source of unity for the living and experiencing of the faith at both the personal and the public levels.

Furthermore, liturgical repetition is a response to the necessity of deepening the significance of ritualised celebration; this, in turn, has the objective of developing and strengthening religious feeling which is aroused by the use of symbols and these symbols are, in themselves, crystallisations of the deepest human emotions. One must not forget that etymologically *to celebrate* means to repeat and that *solemnity* (derived from 'solus annus') refers to an event which is repeated annually. Moreover, ritualised repetition helps to preserve both the personal and the collective memory which makes such a contribution to the processes of identifying individuals and peoples.

It is obvious that the liturgical year constitutes a basic form of Christian instruction. However, the following limitations must be taken into account; the cultural origins of the liturgical year are to be found in Mediterranean countries, it has close ties with agriculture and with traditional crafts, it is characteristic of the Church of Christendom and its celebrations frequently clash with other important dates selected by popular Catholicism and by civil or commercial societies.[29]

(f) Increasing the possibilities of symbolism in worship

Human communication is achieved by means of words and symbols. Speech is not only the communication of ideas or concepts, it is also a 'vocal gesture'. Before a child understands words, it already understands gestures. But, language is written in letters and numbers and to know a language is to be able to decipher. Although all language is symbolic, spoken words are mere sounds—they can be heard but cannot be seen. A symbol is radically a form of non-language and cannot be described as a form of linguistic transcription, either semantically or logically—even metaphorical expressions and metaphors themselves properly belong to the category of word.[30]

In conclusion, we can agree with L. Maldonado 'that the liturgy has to be eminently symbolical and ritualised if it is to make a radical impact on people and be a profound experience, a quasi-mystical sensation, a pleasure and an enjoyment which will render it unforgettable and always eager for renewal'.[31]

(g) The liturgy and its relation to culture

Each and every human group is conditioned and defined by a series of cultural realities related to modes of thinking, norms of conduct and forms of communication. It is not sufficient to affirm that the liturgy is a most important expression of faith; it is at the same time an expression of the culture of a people. It must not be forgotten that the words cult (worship) and culture share the same etymological root; they are derived from *colere* which means to cultivate, to care for, to ennoble or to improve.

The forms of thinking which can be generally categorised under the heading *ideologies* are nowadays not just numerous but sometimes even contradictory. The deliberate omission from the liturgy of this important cultural fact constitutes a serious error and one that creates a measure of dissatisfaction amongst certain critics. The same can be said of social *mores* or customs whether they be upheld, rejected or in the process of decline; they constitute the group of norms of behaviour or conduct which make up, in a rigid or more relaxed way, the structures of any given society. The people who attend a liturgical celebration differ in sex, in age and in levels of culture, they have customs, ideas and convictions that are determined by a thousand and one personal and social factors. Faced with this very wide range of a series of facts defined by civilisation and which condition any society's self-expression and which can be described in a wide sense as *culture*, liturgists adopt two basic attitudes; they either *reject* any adaptation to new cultural forms and so liturgical rites remain rooted in an ever increasingly distant past or they adopt a form of *cultural adaptation* or inculturation by embodying the celebration of the faith in forms of expression which are constantly being up-dated.[32]

The first of these attitudes is reactionary and conservative and forgets that the language of the liturgy never developed independently of a cultural milieu. Indeed, there were times, frequently corresponding to those moments when liturgical texts acquired fixed forms and were committed to writing, when the Church not only adopted profane cultural forms but also contributed to the creation of a distinct culture. Let it suffice to note the influence that religion, culture and even the liturgy have had on popular culture, even up to the present day, in many expressions related to folklore, music, crafts and language. However, it has to be acknowledged that this does not preclude the fact that the Church can become marginal and that Christianity can become increasingly divorced from the context of world culture with the accompanying danger that the liturgy becomes a mere form of subculture.

The second of these attitudes searches out, adopts and incorporates into the language of the liturgy and, consequently, into the language of the faith, expressions taken from contemporary culture. This is done because those present at the Christian assembly are more or less acquainted with the cultural structures of the present day, both at the conceptual level and at the level of symbolic expression. In this way, culture and cult (liturgical worship) grow into a union through a process of cultivation which has properly developed and genuine roots.[33]

Translated by John Angus Macdonald

Notes

1. E. Alberich 'Liturgia e catechesi. La sintesi del mistero cristiano offerta dalla liturgia' *Orientamenti Pedagogici* 13 (1966) 691–713 and *Catequesis y pastoral eclesial* (Madrid 1983) pp. 217–231; J. Aldazábal 'Preguntas a la catequesis desde la liturgia' *Phase* 20 (1980) 255–266; P. H. André 'La Liturgie au coeur de la catéchèse *Catéchistes* 62 (1965) 115–130; A. Cuva 'La liturgia al Sinodo dei Vescovi sulla catechesi. Documentazione e relievi' *Notitiae* 14 (1978) 90–118 and 131–153; I. H. Dalmais 'La Liturgie comme lieu théologique' *La Maison-Dieu* 78 (1964) 97–105; I. H. Dalmais 'La liturgia y el depósito de la fe' in *La Iglesia en oración. Introducción a la liturgia* ed. A. G. Martimort (Barcelona 1964) pp. 256–264; J. Drissen *Liturgische Katechese. Die Liturgie als Strukturprinzip der Katechese* (Frieburg, Basle, Vienna 1965); K. Eguileor 'Liturgia y catequesis' *Liturgia* 24 (1969) 284–298; W. Esser and others *Liturgia y pedagogía en la fe* (Madrid 1969); L. Maldonado 'Catequesis y liturgia' *Catequesis y promoción humana* (Salamanca 1969) 81–92; E. Moeller 'Liturgie et catéchèse au Congrès Liturgique de Hout-halem (29th.–31st. October, 1979)' *Questions Liturgiques* 60 (1979) 135–147; A. Rouet 'Catechese et liturgie, Radiographie d'un débat insuffisant' *La Maison-Dieu* 140 (1979) 7–23; The following articles should also be consulted: 'Liturgical Experience of Faith' *Concilium* 82 (1973); 'Liturgia e catechesi' *Rivista Liturgica* 60 (1973–1975); 'La liturgie, confession de foi' *La Maison-Dieu* 134 (1978); 'Liturgie et catéchèse, en marge du Synode des évêques de 1977' *Questions Liturgiques* 60 (1979/1–2); 'Catéchèse et Liturgie' *La Maison-Dieu* 140 (1979) and 'Liturgia y catequesis' *Phase* 20 (1980) no. 118.

2. O. Rousseau *Histoire du mouvement liturgique. Esquisse historique depuis le début de XIXᵉ siecle jusqu'au pontificat de Pie X* (Paris 1945); W. Trapp *Vorgeschichte und Ursprung der Liturgischen Bewegung* (Regensburg 1940); T. Mass-Ewerd *Liturgie und Pfarrei. Einfluss der Liturgischen Erneuerung auf Leben und Verständnis der Pfarrei in Deutschen Sprachgebiet* (Paderborn 1969).

3. A. G. Martimort 'El doble movimiento de la liturgia: Culto a Dios y Santificación de los hombres' *La iglesia en oración. Introducción a la liturgia* (Barcelona 1964) pp. 221–232; J. Gélineau 'La Pastorale liturgique' *Dans vos assemblées. Sens et pratique de la célébration liturgique* (Paris 1971) I. pp. 4–6.

4. L. Maldonado 'Liturgia' *Conceptos fundamentales de Pastoral* (Madrid 1983) pp. 580–594; E. J. Lengeling 'Liturgia' *Conceptos fundamentales de la Teología* (2nd ed., Madrid 1979) I, pp. 918–941.

5. *Tra le sollecitudine* (22 November 1903); Pius XI *Divini Cultus* (20 November 1928); Pius XII *De musica sacra et de sacra doctrina* (3 September 1958) and *Sacrosanctum Concilium*, nos. 11, 14, 19, 21, 30, 41, 48, 79 and 114.

6. I. Gomá y Tomás, a Canon of the Cathedral Chapter of Barcelona who became Archbishop of Toledo and Primate of Spain. In 1918, in the same year as Romano Guardini edited *The Spirit of the Liturgy*, he published his famous work *El valor educativo de la liturgia católica* which saw three editions published in Barcelona in 1918, 1939 and 1954 respectively.

7. R. Coffy and R. Varro 'La Iglesia, signo de salvacion en medio de los hombres' *Informes presentados a la Asamblea Plenaria del Episcopado Frances, Lourdes, 1971* (Madrid 1976); The Spanish National Secretariate for the Liturgy *Evangelización y sacramento* (Madrid 1975); The

Italian Episcopal Conference *Evangelizzazione, Sacramenti, Promozione umana. Le scelte pastorali della Chiesa in Italia* (Rome 1979).

8. V. Codina 'Presupuestos teológicos para una pastoral sacramental hoy' *Los sacramentos hoy: teología y pastoral* (Madrid 1982) pp. 11–26; L. Maldonado *Iniciaciones a la teología de los sacramentos* (Madrid 1977); C. Traets 'Orientations pour une théologie des sacrements' *Questions Liturgiques* 53 (1972) 97–118.

9. G. Tyrrell *Lex orandi, or Prayer and Creed* (London 1904) and *Lex credendi. A Sequel of Lex orandi* (London 1906); E. Vilanova *La Litúrgia, des de l'ortodoxia i l'ortopraxi* (Barcelona 1981).

10. Audience of 12 December, 1935 granted by B. Capelle and referred to in *La Saint Siège et le mouvement liturgique* (Louvain 1936) 22; A. Bugnini *Documenta pontificia ad instaurationem liturgicae spectantia. 1903–1935* (Rome 1953) pp. 70–71.

11. K. Lehmann 'Gottesdienst als Ausdruck des Glaubens' *Liturgisches Jahrbuch* 30 (1980) 197–214; K. Federer *Liturgie und Glaube. 'Legem credendi lex statuat supplicandi'. Eine theologiegeschichtliche Untersuchung* (Fribourg 1950); P. de Clerck 'Lex orandi, lex credendi. Sens original et avatars historiques d'un adage équivoque' *Questions Liturgiques* 59 (1978) 193–212.

12. G. Lukken 'The Unique Expression of Faith in the Liturgy' in *Concilium* 82 (1973) 11–21 and 'La Liturgie comme lieu théologique irremplaçable' *Questions Liturgiques* 56 (1975) 97–112; S. Marsili 'Liturgia e Teología. Proposta teoretica' *Rivista Liturgica* 59 (1972) 455–473.

13. H. Schürmann 'Neutestamentliche Marginalien zur Frage der Entsackralisierung' *Ursprung und Gestalt* (Düsseldorf 1970) pp. 299–325.

14. *Sharing the Light of the Faith. National Catechetical Directory for the Catholics of the United States* (Washington 1978) p. 22.

15. I. H. Dalmais 'La liturgia y el depósito de la fe' *La Iglesia en oracion* ed. A. G. Martimort (Barcelona 1964) pp. 257 and 259.

16. A.-M. Triacca 'Fides magistra omnium credentium' *La liturgie, expression de la foi* ed. A.-M. Triacca and A. Pistoia, Conférences Saint Serge XXV Semaine d'Etudes liturgiques (Rome 1979) pp. 265–310.

17. R. Coffy 'La Célébration, lieu de l'éducation de la foi' *La Maison Dieu* 140 (1979) 30.

18. A.-M. Triacca, the article cited in note 16, p. 11.

19. *Catechesi Tradendae*, Apostolic Exhortation of John Paul II, 16 October 1979 p. 23.

20. The Italian Episcopal Conference *Il rinovamento della catechesi* (Rome 1970) pp. 130 and 114.

21. *Los documentos de Medellín* (Barcelona 1969) 9 Liturgia, no. 1.

22. *Ibid.* no. 7a.

23. *Documentos de Puebla* (Madrid 1979) no. 901.

24. J.-P. Audet 'La fe y la expresión cultural' *La liturgia después del Vaticano II* ed. J.-P. Jossua and Y. Congar (Madrid 1969) pp. 385–437.

25. C. Floristán and L. Maldonado *Los sacramentos, signos de liberación* (Madrid 1977) pp. 14–15; C. Floristán 'Sakramente und Befreiung' *Prophetische Diakonie. Ferdinand Klostermann zum 70. Geburstag* (Vienna 1977) pp. 292–310.

26. L. Maldonado 'La liturgia entre el hoy y el mañana' in 'Hacia el Vaticano III' *Concilium* 138B (1978) pp. 369–386 (not published in the English edition).

27. C. Floristán 'La predicacion como quehacer pastoral' *Sal Terrae* 66 (1978) 211–217.

28. Y. Congar 'La "Ecclesia" o comunidad cristiana, sujeto integral de la acción liturgica' *La liturgia después del Vaticano II* (Madrid 1969) pp. 279–338.

29. C. Floristán 'Ritmos litúrgicos y ritmos de sociedad' *Phase* 20 (1980) 39–49.

30. A. Vergote 'Gestos y acciones simbólicas en la liturgia' *Concilium* 62 (1971) 198–211.

31. L. Maldonado, the article cited in note 26, p. 380.

32. L. Maldonado *Secularización de la liturgia* (Madrid 1970); R. Panikkar *Culto y secularización* (Madrid 1979).

33. J. Rogues 'La Liturgie et son environnement culturel' *La Maison-Dieu* 146 (1981) 21–38.

John Westerhoff

On Knowing: The Bi-cameral Mind

CHRISTIAN REVELATION is founded upon and assumes a subjective experience of a sacred dimension of reality or to be more precise a relational experience of intimacy with God. Christian theology asserts that through objective reflection it provides an articulation of our present experience of God in the light of past experience. However, while a significant number of persons in the Western world describe experiences of the sort identified as religious by phenomenologists Otto, Van der Leeuw, and Eliade, the experience of God can no longer be considered normative. Indeed, for an increasing number the possibility of an experience of God is questioned.[1] As a result, theological reflections have less meaning and play a less significant role in the formation of belief systems. While this modern phenomenon is less than clear and exceptions to any generalisation are numerous, it is my hypothesis that it results, at least in part, to a functional denial of the bicameral mind by the established Church in our modern era.

Since the sixteenth century, the Church's ecclesiastics in their concern for right thinking and doctrine have had a tendency to make reason both the source of religious knowledge and its judge. While some theologians have asserted the importance of the religious affections and the masses have often become excessively concerned with feelings, the Church's catechetical leaders have typically ignored religious experience and been obsessed with teaching doctrine.[2] For all intents and purposes, therefore, a wedge has been driven between the emotions and belief, between subjective experience and objective reflection, between intuitive and intellectual ways of knowing, between the affective and cognitive domains of the mind, between the right and left lobes of the brain, between the sacred and profane dimensions of reality, between revelation and theology. Due to this unfortunate split, the history of the modern Church in the West is the history of a lay heresy of pietism with its exclusive interest in subjective experience and excessive concern for right feelings in conflict with a clerical heresy of rationalism with its exclusive interest in objective reflection and excessive concern with right thought.

In the light of this history it is essential that we avoid a simplistic notion of religious knowing as either objective or subjective. Religious knowing transcends both. Reason is solely, though importantly, that faculty of the mind which helps us to make intelligible our experience and evaluate what is presented to us through our senses and imaginations. While the ideas which result from this intellectual process influence our experiences of reality, the process of meaning-making is best understood as originating in subjective experience and then moving through the imagination to rational reflection and finally to doctrinal and moral convictions, which in turn condition the nature and character of our experiential awareness.

It is my contention, therefore, that a healthy understanding of religion and human life necessitates an acknowledgment of the bicameral mind a comprehension of its functioning. Let me begin, therefore, with the assertion that there are two interdependent modes of thinking, two interdependent dimensions of consciousness.[3] One, the foundation of most catechetical practice within the established Western Church in modern times, is an intellectual way of knowing, a rational way of thinking, an active mode of consciousness. As such it offers an objective-reflective means to knowledge. Explicit in its concern for product content and dominantly verbal in its mode of expression it is at home in the world of order, structure, and certainty. While linear and argumentative in style, it is best suited for engaging persons in logical analysis, prediction, and control. the alternative and most often neglected in modern catechetical practice is an intuitive way of knowing, an affective way of thinking, a passive mode of consciousness. As such it offers a subjective-experiential means to knowledge. Implicit in its concern for process content and fundamentally non-verbal in its mode of expression it is at home in the world of chaos, anti-structure, and ambiguity. While wholistic and sensuous in style, it is best suited for supporting the imagination, mystery, and discovery. It is the artificial separation of these two modes of consciousness, the depreciation among some of the signative, conceptual, and analytical aspects of life and the benign neglect among others of the symbolic, mythical, imaginative and emotive aspects of life which have contributed to our present religious situation in the Western Church. A religious person has developed fully both modes of consciousness and has learned to integrate their functions. Christian life has a symbolic-signative, mythic-conceputal, imaginative-analytical, informational-emotive character.

We cannot *know* God by objective reflection, but we can *know* God through subjective experience. Objective reflection limits us to the surface of reality and what can be directly confronted through the senses. Subjective experience provides the context for perceiving God's self-disclosure indirectly through the imagination. No one has a direct visual, audial, tactile, savorous, olfactory relationship with God. Yet there are levels of awareness that persons may identify within historical and cultural limitations as an experience of God and through the imagination describe as the 'knowledge of God', a knowledge which is more *felt* meaning than *thought* meaning.[4]

Relevant religious thought is grounded in revelation or the intimate, experiential encounter with the mystery which is God. A metaphorical, poetic, symbolic, mythical relationship to God is prior to any meaningful signative, conceptual, analytical description or explanation. While such experiences need to be named, described, explained and expressed intellectually, Christian life is never solely a matter of giving intellectual assent to a body of propositions or truth claims. Theology is best understood as an orderly reflection on our experience of God. Rational theological thinking is a necessary process of articulating, in a more or less systematic manner, human experience as mediated by our acquired, presumed perceptions of reality.

My plea is that we affirm both the sacred, symbolic, nonrational and mystical as well as the profane, discursive, rationalistic and prosaic dimensions of human life. Piety and doctrine, as well as piety and politics must be reunited. We ought not to ignore the intuitive, the somatic, the perceptual, the mystical sensibilities, the affectional dispositions any more than their opposites. Nevertheless, in a world characterised by their estrangement and a catechetical establishment which has tended to overemphasise one to the exclusion of the other, we need a new emphasis on the intuitive domain, the affections and religious experience. All of life—indeed religion itself—comprises sacred and profane elements. The profane points to the surface of life—the objective dimensions of reality; the sacred points to the depths of life—the subjective dimensions of reality. Throughout history, one or the other is dominant. When the secular dominates, science and philosophical, theological reflection assume greater significance; when the sacred dominates the arts and affective, intuitive experience assume greater significance. Both, of course, are important and in every age the Church needs to seek balance.

While catechesis has an essential rational component we need to be aware that the essential core of Christianity—the experience of God—is in danger of being lost under a cloud of rationalising. At the heart of Christian faith is a non-rational element that cannot be conceptualised or turned into discussive speech, though it can and must be communicated. As Amos Wilder put it, 'Imagination is a necessary component of all profound knowing and celebration; all remembering and realising and anticipating; all faith, hope and love. When imagination fails, doctrines become ossified, witness and proclamation wooden, doxologies and litanies empty, consulation hallow and ethics legalistic.'[5] This emphasis on the imagination in Wilder is not a plea for a shallow aestheticism; it is not intended to ignore rigorous thought and moral action; it is only to acknowledge that 'it is at the level of the imagination that the fateful issues of our new world experience must first be mastered. . . . Before the message there must be the vision, before the sermon the hymn, before the prose the poem, before any new theories there must be the theopoetic.'[6]

Two and a half centuries ago a struggle emerged within the faculty of Saint Thomas' School in Leipzig, an unresolved struggle which still marks a schism in the soul of the Church. It was a conflict over the bicameral mind expressed through a struggle between the school's cantor, Johann Sebastian Bach, and its rector, Johann August Ernesti. Ernesti, a pioneer in the literary, historical, critical study of the Scriptures, believed the students should study more and sing less; Bach thought faith and its musical expressions more important. As Jan Chiapusso put it, 'Here we see the tragic conflict between the last and most mighty musical representative of the age of faith and the younger protagonist of the age of reason and science.'[7] Two epics, two cultures, two understandings were at stake. Ernesti wished to make the study of religion the sole purpose of the school. Bach tried to defend the position that the biblical text was designed to release within the reader an intense sort of spiritual activity: faith. Ernesti chose a rationalistic, analytical, intellectual perspective on knowing, while Bach chose an intuitional, experiential perspective. Since those days, the rationalists, with their emphasis on theological reflection and their interest in the literary, historical, critical method of biblical study, have dominated the Church's catechetical life. This regretful emphasis on intellectual mode of consciousness has contributed to the demise of the intuitional mode and contributed to a sickness in the life of the Church. It is the significance of the world of symbol, myth and ritual that must be recaptured in our day. Religious symbols comprise action symbols—sacraments, narrative symbols—myths or sacred stories, and language symbols—words. The word God only though importantly symbolises the divine, that is, it makes the transcendent present, concrete and effective. Nevertheless, it should not be confused with that to which it points and from which it emerges. Its meaning can only be grasped then filled out by participation in the intuitive subjective experience which underlies it. It is important, however, to note that language symbols also are aids to our participation in the reality to which they point. Still at the heart of the matter is the experience itself and without the experience from which the symbol emerges and to which the symbol points, words remain conceptual verbalisation requiring definition and have no power over present lives.

In 1963, Sir Alister Hardy, the renowned British scientist, in his Gifford Lectures, challenged his fellow scientists to take seriously the fact of religious experience as a central feature of human life. Rising to his own challenge, in 1969 he founded the Religious Experience Research Unit at Manchester College, Oxford. A decade later he published *The Spiritual Nature of Man*, the most seminal analysis of the phenomena of religious experience since that of another Gifford Lecturer, William James. Hardy's successor,

Edward Robinson, in his book *The Original Vision*, reports on their findings concerning the religious experience of childhood. Few existing books offer greater insights for understanding religious life and spiritual awareness, few suggest more radical implications for the reshaping of catechetics.[8] To summarise their findings, a significant number of persons report having religious experiences as young children through nature, the arts, and ritual, but testify that they were unable to name, describe, explain or understand them until much later. Because children could not talk about their experiences, it was assumed they did not have them.

As a result, catechists, following the lead of educators in general, focused their attention on cognition, objective reflection, and decision making (all appropriate, reasonable and necessary for adults), while depreciating the nurturing of the imagination and the affections through the use of the arts and ritual (all appropriate and natural for children) in the catechetical process. The insights reported in *The Original Vision* provides us with a defensible alternative for catechesis with all ages; an alternative that is not just a set of prescriptions for childhood learning, but ones which are essential to the religious life of all persons throughout their human pilgrimage.[9]

Religious thought is grounded in religious experiences. Our conceptualisations of God are grounded in our knowledge of God. Our personal encounter with that ultimate mystery which is God, is expressed, communicated, and nurtured through dance, music, drama, poetry, painting, sculpture, and film; through the stimulation of the imagination and our visual, oral, and kinetic senses. Religious experience and the arts are related; so are religious experience and liturgy. Through ritual—repetitive, symbolic aesthetic actions expressive of the community's story (memory and vision)—our subjective-experiential-intuitive mode of consciousness, the religious imagination and the religious affections are enhanced and enlivened. The distance we have put between ourselves and the arts in the Church has impoverished our religious experience and diminished the effectiveness of both our liturgies and our catechetical ministries.

The arts incarnate our experience of mystery, wonder, and awe; they thereby aid us to encounter the holy or sacred. A number of years ago the College Society for Church Work of the Episcopal Church held a symposium for poets and theologians at the College of Preachers in Washington, D.C. (USA). In a conversation concerning the papers prepared for the gathering, Denise Levertov, a poet, commented that it seemed in a peculiar way that the poets were the believers and the theologians the sceptics. For too long the Church has worried about the relationship between Athens (Greek culture) and Jerusalem (Jewish culture) and neglected the more important question: 'What has Zion (religious life) to do with Bohemia (artistic life)?' My answer is everything!

The function of artistic expression is to illumine and draw us deeper into life's depths. The arts incarnate our experience of mystery, wonder and awe and thereby aid us to encounter the holy or sacred. Without the arts we are cut off from most of the means by which we perceive life's ultimate meaning. As Rudolph Arnheim put it: 'Art is society's most profound reminder that we humans cannot live by bread alone.'[10] The arts both express and nurture our intuitive, affective, responsive mode of consciousness. They remind us that faith precedes theology; that our knowledge of God is prior to our conceptualisation of God. They help us to understand that our sense of God's presence is an intuitive, affective experience. Our personal encounter with that ultimate mystery which is God is nurtured, expressed and communicated through dance, painting, music, sculpture, poetry, and drama especially as they are expressed in liturgy.

Religious life and artistic life go hand-in-hand. Religion belongs to the sphere of the unsayable, the absurd, the world of nonsense which if it is to be put into words at all, must use metaphorical images, symbol words, poetry. That is why catechesis is dependent on the arts. Only if the religious affections and the arts become basic to catechesis will persons acquire those perceptions and share those experiences which make it possible for us to be fully human in community. Only through the imagination will we gain those insights and understandings necessary for human survival. We have for too long neglected the development of both our conscious and unconscious minds. We have limited our human capacities, we have neglected our deeper consciousness and estranged ourselves from our creative selves. Until we can restore the religious affection to this proper role in human life we will remain captive to our conditioning and separated from meaningful relationships with God, self, neighbour, and nature. Human individual and corporate life is at stake in the estrangement of Zion and Bohemia. Their reunion may well be the greatest challenge facing catechesis in our day.[11]

Religious experience is nurtured and stimulated by the aesthetic especially as it is participated in and expressed through liturgy which at its best is an art activity making religious awareness, the religious imagination, the experience of the holy or sacred possible. The liturgy both expresses and nurtures religious experience. In the explicit catechesis of the liturgy, the Christian story in the form of symbolic narrative (the foundation of Christian doctrine) is shared and enacted in the context of experiential-affective worship. In the implicit catechesis of the liturgy our perceptions, attitudes, dispositions and values are shaped through participation in its symbolic actions. Within this essentially intuitive event children and adults are offered the foundational experience necessary for Christian faith and life. For example, our characters, which are comprised of perceptions, dispositions, attitudes and values, are shaped through processes of inculturation in a story-formed liturgical community of faith. Of course there is more. Our consciences, an activity of whole persons (thinking, feeling and willing) in conscious loyalty to Jesus, making moral judgments on what is a faithful action in a particular historical and cultural situation need to be educated through the development of intellectual reflective processes. The nature of the character is dependent upon an intuitive way of knowing, the conscience on an intellectual way of knowing. These dual processes of formation and education comprise catechesis. They are dependent upon each other, though in both developmental and chronological sequence character is formed prior to the education of conscience, just as the intuitive way of knowing is prior to the intellectual.

A new awareness of the visual, artistic, imaginative, associative, and relational activities of the brain, therefore, cannot be permitted to dull or limit our concern for speech, logic, cognitive reasoning, analysis, and linear activities. To be religious the intuitive and intellectual ways of knowing must be developed to the fullest possible extent. However, having overemphasised the intellectual, the Church today needs to give special attention to the intuitive. While always remembering that to be human both hemispheres of our bicameral mind must be developed, the nurturing of religious experience through sensualisation in the learning process demands attention.

Notes

1. Lois Dupre 'Spiritual Life in a Secular Age' *Daedalus* 111:1 (1982) 21–31.

2. Hermann Hesse's novel *Beneath the Wheel* (New York 1968), based in part on Hesse's own experience, constitutes an acknowledgment of the duality of human nature and an attack on educational systems that foster the intellect to the detriment of emotion.

3. See Robert Ornstein *The Psychology of Consciousness* (San Francisco 1972).

4. See Michael Polanyi *The Tacit Dimension* (Chicago 1966).

5. Amos Niven Wilder *Theopoetic* (Philadelphia 1976) p. 2.

6. *Ibid.* p. 2.

7. Jan Chiapusso *Bach's World* (New York 1968) p. 43.

8. Edward Robinson *The Original Vision* (New York 1983).

9. An exception to this tendency is *Aesthetic Dimensions of Religious Education* ed. Gloria Durka and Joanmarie Smith (New York 1979) and Cathleen Fischer *The Inner Rainbow: The Imagination in the Christian Life* (New York 1983).

10. Rudolph Arnheim *Art and Visual Perception* (Berkeley 1969) p. 212.

11. See John Westerhoff and John Eusden *The Spiritual Life: Learning East and West* (New York 1983).

Norbert Mette

The Christian Community's Task in the Process of Religious Education

IN THE discussion of religious education and catechetics increased attention has for some time now been devoted to the task of the community in the process of transmitting the faith. 'Community catechesis' and 'community education' are at the centre of consideration of the ideas involved.[1] Turning in this way to the community as the locus of education is accompanied by a change in perspective in the traditional understanding and in its practical expression: these saw learning predominantly as an affair of children and young people and thus localised it in the phase of formal education. This is the thesis which will be expanded in what follows. The greater prominence given to the duties of the community involves more implications and consequences than merely adding one more institution to those already concerned with handing on the faith or giving a different emphasis to what they have been taken as signifying. It is rather a question of realising and implementing the business of handing on the faith more clearly as an inter-active and social process and thus of correcting what had become too individualistic and privatised a way of looking at it.

It would thus be too simplistic merely to put together a list of possible tasks to be undertaken by the community. Rather it is indispensable to ascertain what are the decisive reasons for the community now being attributed greater importance in the context of handing on the faith. Hence the considerations that follow draw on the analyses of sociology and attempt to combine their findings with the insights of theology and the theory of religious education in such a way that the close connection becomes obvious between the community and handing on the faith, a connection that will become even more significant in the future.

1. THE EPOCH-MARKING SIGNIFICANCE OF THE COMMUNITY AS THE AGENT OF HANDING ON THE FAITH

If Christian faith has to do with the disclosure, interpretation and deepening of fundamental experiences involved in being human, handing it on is very much dependent on whether the possible conditions exist for such experiences. As long as an environment marked by Christianity was predominant, this problem hardly arose. Anyone who grew up in a society of this kind unhesitatingly came into contact with statements about life by

69

Christians and the Church. The situation is different once it cannot be ignored that there has been a fundamental change in the social conditions of life and that familiar religious traditions have been strongly affected by this. It can no longer be taken for granted that the rising generation will be made familiar with the heritage of experiences preserved in these traditions. In fact, it is increasingly a case of a break in tradition. We cannot list here all the factors responsible for this development. From the point of view of our understanding of the process of socialisation what emerges as particularly significant is the fact that the handing on of Christianity is dependent on social conditions which are less and less able to predominate in modern industrial society on account of its predominant pattern of relationship and organisation:[2]

(a) According to F. X. Kaufmann handing on the Christian faith 'presupposes a suitable style of interaction dominated by features which are not functionally specific but which involve the mutual recognition of identity'.[3] What therefore are indispensable are close-knit and durable networks of social relationships in which those involved can still mutually recognise each other as 'complete human beings' without already being reduced to partial roles.

(b) To a not unappreciable extent, acceptance of the faith results from processes of interpersonal identification in networks of this kind: by meeting actual people who convincingly try to live as Christians in their everyday life and are ready to discuss this with others and to bear witness to it to them.

(c) Beyond this, Christianity's strength in the life of society seems to prevail if it can be realised in a variety of intellectual orientations and social movements and in this way admits different forms of personal appropriation.

If one asks where in contemporary society social conditions of this kind can be found the first answer will be the family. It offers comparatively favourable conditions for 'reaching that intensity of interaction that makes lasting identifications possible'.[4] But the family's capacity to achieve all this should not be overestimated:

(i) It possesses only a limited ability to bring into play the forms of social intercourse that favour it in view of the dominant type of social relationships that are regulated according to the principle of formal organisation and are thus organised on an anonymous basis. On the contrary, because it often has to pay the price of acting for its members as the collecting ring for problems that have arisen elsewhere, its situation has become so precarious that it needs to be supported by larger networks of greater scope.

(ii) However irreplaceable the primary relationships are for the person growing up, what is important for the child and particularly for the young person is to be able to meet people outside the parental home who live, talk and act on the basis of the Christian faith.

(iii) The possibilities of a pluralism of Christian experiences of the world are naturally limited within the privatised nuclear family. Usually the wider network of relations offers too low a durability and density of communication. For this reference can most easily be made to the circle of friends with whom members of a family are in touch.

The problem thus is 'where today social situations can still be found of sufficient density and duration for personal relationships intense enough for the transmission of Christian values to be able to arise in them'.[5] The Church is not able to provide this to the extent that it is organised as a large-scale institution within society. It experiences the same fate as other organisations: it may be publicly present but can only to a limited extent exert influence on how people lead their personal lives. 'The public sphere and that of how people lead their personal lives have today diverged too far for a large-scale organisation belonging to the public sphere to be able to transmit determinative guidance for the conduct of personal life.'[6] The possibilities of discovering meaning are linked to the availability of relatively comprehensible patterns of life.

These considerations argue in favour of locating the social form best adapted to the transmission of the faith more or less between the family on one side and, on the other side, society—including the Church, to the extent that it bears the marks of a large-scale organisation. This points us in the direction of the parish community or congregation. It is understood by sociology as providing precisely that social form that goes beyond the scope of the family but still represents a pattern of life that can be grasped and is hardly touched by the process of social differentiation. 'Its structural situation at the point of intersection between the public and private spheres makes it the privileged social locus and medium for the handing on of Christian insights for the future.'[7]

It is precisely here that the community's epoch-marking significance in the present conditions of Church and society is to be found. In the process of handing on the faith it occupies a particularly valuable position which, with the exception of the epoch of the early Church, is in this form new. This does not mean that the other institutions of socialisation used to hand on Christianity can be declared superfluous. But the family and the school, to the extent that they still make a contribution, are directed towards being able to point to loci where people try to live in common on the basis of the inspiration of the Gospel, or towards themselves participating in this. Doubtless the manifestation of the Church as an institution which extends beyond the level of the individual parish community represents an important factor in the handing on of Christianity under the conditions of modern society; but if the institutional level does not remain linked back to the possibility of living experiences in the community, the offers of meaning that it transmits threaten to take on a character specific to the system and thus to become distanced from the meaning of the individual's life as this can be interpreted biographically.[8]

The epoch-marking significance of the community nevertheless extends beyond the problems of handing on Christianity in the narrower sense. The activation of networks of social relationships as represented by the parish community is also rich in consequences to the extent that it makes feasible the establishment of connections between the family and society, between the private and the public sphere—connections which to a considerable extent have been lost or destroyed but whose lack is beginning meanwhile to have a disastrous effect, especially in the field of the conduct of personal life. To a certain extent this involves the community in a critical function with regard to society, at least when in what it does it does not confine itself simply to compensating for the problem of social integration that arises in modern society because of its complex structure of organisation, but opens up possibilities of organising oneself in which patterns of identity are no longer prescribed but can be discovered and tested jointly by those involved. Communities of this kind as loci of value-forming and norm-building communication are a significant potential transformation or innovation for Church and society: the reshaping of one's life-style that is becoming ever more urgent in view of various lurking crises (we need only think of the population explosion, the shortage of foodstuffs, the shortage of energy and of raw materials, and increasing isolation) can be worked out experimentally and tested in a variety of ways.[9]

2. THE FORMATION OF THE COMMUNITY AS A PROCESS OF LEARNING

These sociological indications find a remarkable echo in recent discussions of the theology of the parish community. The fact that the community has become such a central theme of theology can be interpreted as a reaction to the social change sketched out above. As has already been indicated, the feature of learning as a fundamental dimension of community behaviour emerges ever more strongly in the context of this discussion, and not just in the obvious sense of an increasing number of educational projects being included in communities' programmes. The fundamental value that is ascribed to learning in the context of the community is to be expounded in a twofold perspective:[10]

(a) The Christian faith and its transformation are fundamentally connected with the ability to learn and grasp new possibilities of life as these have been offered by God to men and women and manifested unsurpassably in Jesus Christ. Anyone who involves himself or herself with this faith in the visible social shape that it takes on in a particular kind of interpersonal human relationships (i.e. those brought about by the spirit of this Jesus) is enabled on the basis of the mutual acceptance he or she experiences to become a man or woman who in solidarity with others learns to shape the joint history of their lives responsibly. Learning to believe is thus connected in a very elementary sense with learning to live: what is characteristic is that it finds its fulfilment in a common mode of behaviour. In this sense the community forms a constitutive dimension in the process of handing on the faith.

(b) This reference to the community as the locus of learning how to be a Christian nevertheless has its dangers. The fact that Christians come together is no guarantee of a coming together in the sense of the Gospel: here too the compulsions of objective circumstances and the roles people play can flourish in all sorts of ways. Communities must therefore continually strive to become contexts in which people can jointly learn and live their vocation to become responsible agents. The central characteristic of the community in this sense is therefore that it should form a learning process that is continually open to the spirit of God.

The radical consequences that flow from this become manifest when we ascertain the biblical concepts that characterise this process of learning and that denote its goal and direction: 'conversion' and 'discipleship'.[11] A community's process of learning is not exhausted simply by the achievement of adaptation or even attaining the optimum. Instead, the community is the place where people jointly learn and practise what 'conversion' and 'discipleship' mean; and in the process of this learning and practising this place itself is continually changed, in that it lets itself become more and more visibly marked by the promised fullness of life. What dawned in Jesus's proclamation and behaviour and was ratified in his being raised up by God should find its continuation in the community: the creation of that healing environment in which God's mercy becomes visibly incarnate and manifest and his reign or kingdom gains ground. The new orientation given to one's life which is offered and made possible in faith and which involves a revision of one's familiar ways finds in the community the locus of its social obligation. Consequently transmitting the faith is an extremely social procedure which cannot succeed in isolation from the community. It is here that one can find, throughout one's life and in mutual solidarity, the experience of unconditional acceptance and being able to trust each other that God has made possible—an atmosphere that gives one the courage and the readiness continually to learn afresh how to be a disciple and follow Christ, how to achieve conversion and *metanoia*.

This process of learning in the community and as a community must not on any account be understood as something that can only take place in an artificially created world apart. Rather, it finds its place in the reality of society with all its contradictions. Thus the community finds itself automatically in the midst of the struggle to decide which demands of this learning process are to be directed to people in view of the existing and likely tasks of individual and social formation today, and it must ask itself what contribution it can make towards this.

In this context what is being underlined with increasing urgency is how much depends both for the individual man or woman and for mankind as a whole on the development of a process of re-thinking which results ultimately in a different way of dealing with nature, with other people and with oneself—different in the sense of being guided not by a concern for domination and exploitation but by consideration and reconciliation. The 'anthropological revolution' that is called for here has, as J. B. Metz has repeatedly emphasised, something very profoundly to do with the biblical demand for a 'conversion of the heart';[12] and hence communities cannot dispense themselves from taking part in this process of cultural and political change. They cannot simply limit themselves to being able to experience and celebrate together a meaning which establishes identity and which is not encountered anywhere else merely in some niche or corner of society. Rather their particular opportunity consists in the fact that the transformation of consciousness exercised within them—a transformation which crystallises out among other things in a new style of associating with and dealing with each other—does not remain without consequences precisely because, as sketched out above, it is situated at the boundary between the private and the public realm and hence can be an exemplary social locus 'where political life becomes personal in its new moral claims and personal life reaches out to political life in its radical perplexities'.[13]

Nevertheless it should be realistically understood that the reality of the Church only corresponds to all this to a limited extent. But promising initiatives are to be found in the *communautés de base* or small grassroots groups that are increasingly spreading. What is verified in them is what W. Bartholomäus has formulated as follows: 'The key to all future activity in religious education is the power of conviction of the communities which on the basis of many people's varied efforts proceed to realize a way of living everyday life which is shaped through and through by Christianity, however fragmentary and despondent this may be. This springs from the will to change oneself and not others. Against this background of experience being a Christian has an opportunity of scandalizing parents and children, pupils and teachers once again.'[14]

3. LEARNING IN THE COMMUNITY AND LEARNING AS A COMMUNITY—WAYS TO A COMMON
FAITH

The discussion so far has made it clear that the process of learning in which the faith is transmitted shows definite characteristics which do not conform completely to current ideas about the theory of learning:

(*a*) Learning the faith is a total process of learning that involves the whole man or woman. The invitation to discipleship and the challenge to conversion cannot be compartmentalised but affect all spheres of life. The aim of learning the faith is becoming a responsible agent, is man's or woman's 'integral liberation'. This rules out every form of compulsion and manipulation.

(*b*) Learning the faith is a process that lasts as long as life itself: it follows the course of human development and encourages it by continually challenging one to become personally aware of and appropriate the fullness of life with the promise it offers.

(*c*) Learning the faith is a process that transcends the generations: it is a mutual process in which those involved learn from each other.[15] What is characteristic is its reversal of the usual situation of teaching and learning: before God children, teenagers and grown-ups are linked in a common situation of learning. While the various modes of belief of the different age-ranges are given equal realisation side by side, something of the fullness of the gospel's inspiration becomes visible.

(*d*) Learning the faith is a process of learning in solidarity. It takes place when faith and life are shared among each other and the experiences they bring are also shared among each other and interpreted jointly in the light of the biblical message.

(*e*) Learning the faith is a committed process of learning. Learning to grasp the possibilities of life given by God makes one sensitive to everyone deprived of the elementary right of living and of bringing one's life to fulfilment.

(*f*) Learning the faith is an innovatory process of learning. It does not simply limit itself to instruction in current values and norms. Rather it arouses at the same time the ability to examine them to see whether they make human life possible and in certain cases to change them.[16]

All these predicates amount to the fact that handing on the faith is very much a social process that is linked to corresponding experiences in one's association with other people. Learning the faith and forming the community are to a certain extent the two sides of one and the same coin.

From this it is clear that the point above all of plans for approaches in teaching and for individual methods is to form communities in which attempts at living the Christian life in a way that corresponds to the demands of today can jointly be learned and tested. The present crisis in handing on the faith is to a considerable extent linked to the fact that there is too little opportunity of pointing to communities in which what arises from the practical demands of discipleship is made manifest: that 'qualitative change in one's perception of reality and one's common involvement with it, just like a transformation of people's dealings with each other,' that is inspired by the Gospel.[17] Setting such a substantial process of learning in motion and thereby contributing towards solving the urgent problems affecting society and individuals can, as has been shown, be seen as an epoch-marking challenge which Christian communities have to face themselves with and which they offer favourable conditions for making the most of. When this challenge is accepted with commitment, when they consistently venture on learning jointly to live and to believe, then the problem of handing the faith on to the next generation ought to a certain extent to solve itself.

Translated by Robert Nowell

Notes:

1. See, besides John Paul II *Catechesi tradendae*, especially §§ 25 and 67, the following examples of official Church statements in West Germany: (Catholic) 'Das katechetische Wirken der Kirche' in *Gemeinsame Synode der Bistümer in der Bundesrepublik Deutschland. Offizielle Gesamtausgabe*, ed. L. Bertsch and others (Freiburg 1977) II pp. 37–97; (Protestant) *Zusammenhang von Leben, Glauben und Lernen. Empfehlungen zur Gemeindepädagogik*, put forward by the Board for Education and Formation of the Evangelische Kirche in Deutschland (Gütersloh 1982).

2. On what follows see K. Gabriel ' "Messung" pastoralen Erfolgs—religions—soziologisch' in *Erfolgreiche—nicht-erfolgreiche Gemeinde* ed. J. Horstmann (Paderborn 1981) pp. 84–94; K. Gabriel 'Christentum und Industriegesellschaft' in *Person—Gruppe—Gesellschaft* (Hildesheim 1981) pp. 31–43; F.-X. Kaufmann *Kirche begreifen* (Freiburg 1979); F.-X. Kaufmann 'Gesellschaftliche

Bedingungen der Glaubensvermittlung', in *Sozialisation—Identitätsfindung—Glaubenserfahrung* ed. G. Stachel and others (Zürich/Einsiedeln/Cologne 1979) pp. 67–100.

3. F.-X. Kaufmann 'Gesellschaftliche Bedingungen', the article cited in note 2, at p. 97.

4. *Ibid.* p. 82.

5. *Ibid.* p. 97.

6. K. Gabriel, the work cited in note 2, at p. 87.

7. *Ibid.* p. 88.

8. See K. Gabriel, the article cited in note 2, especially pp. 40–41.

9. For more detail see N. Mette and H. Steinkamp *Sozialwissenschaften und Praktische Theologie* (Düsseldorf 1983) especially chapter 4.

10. On what follows, see among others W. Bartholomäus 'Das Lernen von Christsein' in *Diakonia* 14 (1983) 25–33; J. Bommer 'Lernort Gemeinde: Gemeinden lernen ihren Glauben' in *Katechetische Blätter* 108 (1983) 114–121; R. Zerfass 'Predigt und Gemeinde' in *Trierer Theologische Zeitschrift* 92 (1983) 89–104.

11. See J. B. Metz *Jenseits bürgerlicher Religion* (Munich/Mainz 1980) and his *Spuren des Messianischen* (Munich/Mainz 1983).

12. See Metz *Jenseits*, especially pp. 60ff., 99–100.

13. See J. B. Metz *Unterbrechungen* (Gütersloh 1981) p. 18.

14. W. Bartholomäus, the article cited in note 10, 33; see also E. Schillebeeckx 'Erfahrung und Glaube', in *Christlicher Glaube in moderner Gesellschaft* ed. F. Böckle and others fasc. 25 (Freiburg 1980) pp. 73–116, especially pp. 112ff.

15. This aspect is stressed in particular by K. E. Nipkow *Grundfragen der Religionspädagogik* III; *Gemeinsam leben und glauben lernen* (Gütersloh 1982) especially pp. 30–43 and 233–261.

16. See the declaration of the Synod of Bishops in Rome, 1972, on Justice to the World, § 52.

17. H. Peukert 'Sprache und Freiheit' in *Ethische Predigt und Alltagsverhalten* ed. F. Kamphaus and R. Zerfass (Munich/Mainz 1977) pp. 44–75: the quotation comes from p. 45.

Wolfgang Bartholomäus

Being a Christian in the Church and the World of Tomorrow

AS I was working on this article I continually found myself wondering whether there was any point in addressing the topic dealt with in this issue. Surely anything we say about Christian existence in tomorrow's church and tomorrow's world will be no more than vague guesswork. Is there any other way of knowing the future apart from extrapolating from the present? Such extrapolation only prolongs the present; it cannot foresee the possibility of historical hiatus and of unexpected developments. What possible methodological justification can there be, therefore, for saying anything at all that will be meaningful?

And there are problems of content too. Faced with the global nuclear threat, can we assume that there *will* be a world of tomorrow? And what of the human beings who have to cope with this threat over a long period: will their anxieties increase or will their ability to find meaning be renewed? What will tomorrow's economic conditions be like? What will be the cultural situation, the political structure, the religious form of society? And if there *is* a world of tomorrow, will there still be Christians and churches? Or will they be totally annihilated in the onward march of secularisation? In the face of the global challenge of tomorrow's world, will tomorrow's Christians and churches suffer extinction or will they recover their strength? What is the social and theological context, therefore, in which we can ask about being a Christian in the Church and the world of tomorrow?

The very fact that we can raise and pursue questions such as these is evidence of confidence in the future. Although for the first time man has access to such destructive potential that he is able totally to annihilate himself, our world is still the object of the promised new world of God. Although the idea of secularisation (which, as an explanation of the religious situation, is of questionable validity) envisages de-christianisation, a secular world order and a post-Christian future, God still remains the Lord of this future.

Here then are a few observations on the question: What are the *guiding perspectives* within which Christian faith can be handed on to the next generation? Guiding perspectives are at work in all human actions. It is when we become aware of them that we are able to act reflectively. These remarks are intended to facilitate such awareness. I am not aiming to compel anyone to adopt any particular guiding perspective.

In fact I ought to speak in the plural all the time, for there will not be one Christian existence in tomorrow's one Church and one world. We cannot expect uniformity in the future, nor would it be desirable in either Church or world. The future which lies before us is characterised by a pluralism which could only be eliminated by totalitarian force, which no one wants to see. Consequently we must understand this multiplicity as setting the stage for freedom. I hope I shall be pardoned for pursuing my remarks in the singular, i.e., with a view primarily to the situation in the Federal Republic of Germany.

1. THE CONTENT OF FAITH

What will the Christian of the future believe? Here any quick answer is bound to be trivial. Of course tomorrow's Christian too will believe what the scriptures and the ancient creeds profess to be the Church's faith. By fundamentally identifying himself with a Church, he shares in this Church's faith. But what is the faith of the churches? I reply: What they proclaim as faith. But this has not been the same at all times. The history of ecclesial proclamation, in preaching and catechesis, shows that, in response to the demands of the times, particular elements were stressed, particular didactic profiles were drawn, all claiming to be based on and situated within the framework of scripture and the creeds. We can definitely say there is a material historicity to faith.

Moreover, in so far as Christians not only participate in the faith of their Church, but also have their own personal history of faith for which they are responsible, they themselves give it a special accentuation. Indeed, there is much to be said for the idea that it is only by doing this that they can keep faith alive. Then as well as the objective development of faith there is the person's subjective faith-history; he must choose. Not that he can reject this or that, but some selection is unavoidable. Christians of all ages have apparently always looked for their own special approach to faith.

(a) The dispute about catechetical formulas

Recently the dispute about the content of faith presented in proclamation has broken out afresh. Cardinal Josef Ratzinger, in an address given in January 1983 in Paris and Lyons which attracted much attention and vociferous criticism, demanded that the transmission of faith in catechetics should return to its traditional form, i.e., the four classical pillars of catechetics, the Creed, the Our Father, the Ten Commandments and the Sacraments. Ratzinger observes that the Roman Catechism of 1566 held that these formulas expressed the dimensions of Christian existence. They show what the Christian has to believe (Creed), to hope (Our Father) and to do (Ten Commandments as the interpretation of the modes of love), and indicate the life-situation in which all this is firmly rooted (Sacraments and the Church).[1] Here the Christian of the future is envisaged as someone who has learned the central catechetical articles and has made them his own in the dimensions of his life.

Ratzinger expressly emphasises that the Bible cannot be the direct substance of faith's transmission. Rather, faith is communicated and revealed in and through these foundational articles. The catechism should form the core of catechesis. For its basic structure must arise out of the logic of faith. And the latter is as old as the early Christian catechumenate, i.e., as old as the Church itself. Faced with the theo-logic of faith, the narrative logic of the Bible (not to mention the psycho-logic and socio-logic of how faith is acquired) must take second place.

In opposing a catechesis which, in his view, no longer presents the traditional faith of the Church, Ratzinger is attacking a mode of Christian existence which aims to get by without a knowledge of these foundational catechetical articles. This anxiety has been shared by State and Church authorities from the time of Charlemagne at least until Martin Luther and Peter Canisius. The believer was seen as a person well versed in these articles.

In crass terms—and this was often regarded as the norm—it meant that he must know them by heart.

What makes Ratzinger's complaint questionable is the fact that he has made it at a time when, by contrast with the European middle ages, there is no longer a social basis for it, nor for the challenge which stems from it. There no longer exists a Christendom uniting everyone and affirmed by everyone as their common context. Moreover, Ratzinger has missed this fact: wherever this common basis of catechetical transmission was not yet established or had ceased to operate, wherever society's de-christianisation or non-Christian nature was at least contemplated, catechesis was supplied with a different content. Thus there was the doctrine of the 'two ways' in primitive catechesis (*Didache*); in the developed form of adult catechumenate in Augustine we find the recounting of salvation history (*De catechizandis rudibus*). Linking up with this latter tradition (Fleury, Gruber, Hirscher, May, Jungmann, Arnold), in periods of missionary proclamation, we find many and varied attempts to evolve a catechesis which follows the course of biblical history, i.e., oriented to the biblical texts. Then there are the most recent attempts to put forward a proclamation which both interprets and transforms the experiences and conflicts of contemporary man, from the point of view of and in the power of the Gospel (catechism of Don Mazzi, Dutch Catechism, the catechism of the peasants of Solentiname).[2]

The demand for unequivocal articles of faith, oriented to the Church's dogma, which has been expressed in the recent call for a reinstatement of the traditional catechetical formulas, is aimed both at securing the Church's identity in history and at guaranteeing its deposit of faith. Both these intentions are right; both are important. But the attempt to achieve this by going back to the catechetical formulas looks more like a nostalgic dream than a response to given realities accurately perceived.

(b) Demonstrating the relevance of faith

Those who are less interested in the Church as an institution and its preservation than in the people in it; those who are more committed to enabling the Church to carry out its mission of bringing meaning and salvation than to ensuring its survival; those who see identity not in identical formulas but in the identical power manifested in what they achieve—all such people are primarily concerned that, in the future, the liberating impulses of the Gospel shall take effect and flow into the language and praxis of proclamation. The truth of the Gospel is shown in its power to illuminate and to transform the experiences and conflicts of men. That is why it is so important to recount and celebrate stories of faith (from the Bible and from the lives of the saints). What is crucial for Christian existence in the future is not that the catechetical formulas should be preserved (though they ought not to disappear from memory) but that people should find meaning, hope should be planted, and love should be made possible in the power of the God of Jesus Christ. What we must do is to find appropriate formulas for the particular age in which we live, so that the power of faith, which liberates people into the sphere of meaning, hope and love, can attain clarity of expression in harmony with the tradition of the church.

The faith of future Christians will lay hold of the Gospel's psychical and social influence. This is only possible if the Gospel is explicated 'in terms of normal life' and by reference to one's own life-history.[3] Faith's rationale is no longer based solely on consonance with tradition. Now it endeavours to expound the Gospel by showing how, within personal and social history, it sets people free (to embrace meaning, hope and love), and by enabling others to experience this for themselves.

Thus the faith of future Christians exists where people experience the liberating influence, in personal life and in society, of the God of Jesus Christ. This influence is recounted in stories of faith and celebrated in worship. It does not reduce revelation to the level of affirmation of present reality. The tough resistance offered by revelation is shown precisely by its ability to smash life's meaningless succession of moments and smooth functioning. For most people, living under conditions of individual and social unfreedom, liberation always means change as well. In the future, faith will not be seen in terms of an intellectual profile but as the soteriological power of the Gospel.

2. BEING A CHRISTIAN IN THE CHURCH

'There is no faith without Church'.[4] This maxim is by no means unambiguous. It can imply that no one comes to faith without having this faith mediated to him by those who have preceded him in faith (Church as that which mediates the Gospel). It may mean that believers cannot exist, theologically speaking and in fact, apart from a continually realised relationship to the Church and, within it, to a particular community (Church as the believer's life space). Hence, naturally, faith implies that believers have an explicit relationship to an ecclesial community, for it is always a faith shared with others, and the God-relation involved in it does not isolate a person from his fellow men; it opens him up to them. The proclamation of faith proceeds on the basis that once faith has been received, it will be lived in the community of the Church.

All the same it seems that this relationship of believers to the Church, necessary as it appears to be, manifests very diverse forms.

(a) National or community Church?

A debate has been going on in the area of practical theology as to whether the Church of the future is or should be a Church of the nation or of a community. The debate has been concerned primarily with the European situation, of course, and its shape has been determined by Europe's Christian history. The idea of the Church as community has gained definition. This community expects each baptised person to have come to a well thought-out decision in faith, to participate intensively in the life of the community, and to be committed to social action on behalf of people. This model was formulated in deliberate opposition to a 'national' Christianity. Here Christians are subject to particular legally formulated prescriptions in terms of religious practice, but they are all regarded as members of the Church even if they seldom have any contact with it, i.e., at the outset of their lives (baptism), in the middle (worship, church tax, marriage) and at the end (funeral). In national Christianity the fact of being baptised creates a poorly developed sense of membership of an institution. This institution demonstrates its existence by those who represent it, the office-bearers (the pope, bishops and priests). By contrast, in the community there is a sense of belonging, a will to belong to a group of people who come together in a shared interest.

Both models of the Church see it primarily as an institution into which believers are to be gathered. It is a centripetal field of force; all its energy presses towards a centre; from outside inwards (the community), from below upwards (national Church). In both cases the principle of self-preservation is more evident than that of self-abandonment. Critics speak of an ecclesial 'self-realisation neurosis' with regard to both models.

(b) Church as sign

The contrary view sees the Church as symbolising the cause of Jesus, namely, freedom from all manner of slavery, freedom for universal community—a freedom willed by God and made possible in him. In the Church what we have is the utopia of God's new world, already present and alive in signs, changing the personal lives and social environment of all people in the direction of freedom and communication. In this context the role of the institution or the group is purely instrumental. They are necessary to maintain the vitality of the cause of Jesus. But its real life is to be seen neither in terms of administration by members of a hierarchically controlled institution (national Church), nor in the enthusiasm for participation and commitment in a 'democratic' Christian community (community). It is to be seen in the realisation of communicative freedom in personal lives and in the world community. This is what being a Christian means. The Church, which serves as an instrument to this end, is organised according to the plurality of Christian forms. There are groups and individuals, the committed and the aloof, office-bearers and laypeople, core-communities and peripheral groups: in their expectations and relationships they bring about what God wills and makes possible, i.e., freedom in a context of communication, relationships which inspire liberation. This means that much bureaucracy and hierarchic alienation can be dispensed with.

I foresee that the future will bring an increasing diversity of ways in which people will belong to the Church. The Church itself will become the sign of and the platform for freedom. What unites the Church is not its hierarchical structure, nor the responsible action of committed members (although both of these exist and are necessary in different degrees). What unites the Church is the inspiring power found in those who proclaim and celebrate the Gospel, who are its heralds and proponents, but who give up all claim to control its influence.

3. COMMUNITY—WHERE FAITH IS TRANSMITTED

There can be no doubt that in future, if Christian existence is to be handed on, it will be handed on in the community. People may object that in the past it was transmitted in other ways: in the middle ages it took place within the world of Christendom (painting, sculpture, Mass, processions, holydays, feast days, *biblia pauperum*, the dance of death, catechism tables and the commandments as a painted frieze, medals and reliquaries, stations of the cross and mystery plays: everything worked together like 'catechetical visual aids', impressing on people, through the eye, things that could scarcely have penetrated more deeply through the ear). In Protestantism, at the beginning of modern times, it took place within the home (the home catechism); in Catholicism in the context of school and parish rooms (Christian doctrine); since the beginning of the nineteenth century in the school religion class; and then, increasingly, within the middle-class family.

However, no one disputes the fact that people can only become Christians as and when they encounter other Christians. The kind of Christianity presented through the media, on which the churches seem to be relying more and more (i.e., televised services, radio sermons, church information in VDU form) may stimulate a certain amount of interest. But it is unsuitable as a means for transmitting faith. Here, effectiveness is seen exclusively in terms of publicity. A further obstacle lies in the ambivalence of all the media, which at the same time both mediate and interpose themselves; they both inform and hold aloof. Direct contact with people is necessary if others are to become Christians. For people are not only models of faith: it is contact with them that creates the emotional and psycho-social conditions with which faith is involved.

This applies equally to societies which have no Christian past and to the post-Christian European society of the future. In the latter case many traces may remain, in psychic and social structures, of its religious and Christian past. But in general it will become increasingly independent of it; its religious memory will fade and it will become incapable of religious experience. Hence the necessity of fields of experience at a community level to transmit and promote Christian existence.

The problem of the family

It is well known that Church leaders have always paid great attention to marriage and the family and to ways of maintaining and shaping them (although throughout the Church's history it has been marriage, rather than the family, which has been at the focus of interest); but however much they may have been concerned with the happiness of those involved, they were also strongly motivated by their expectation that the family would be the transmitter of Christian faith. This hope is intensified today. It is expressed in theological and pastoral terms in the idea of the 'house church', which has been applied to the family more and more frequently ever since Vatican II.[5] Some people even assert that the church's destiny lies entirely with the family: 'The chances of today's Church surviving are almost entirely in the hands of the house churches'.[6]

But it is not simply a question of practical theology whether this manner of speaking, with the expectations it has of the family, is justified. The New Testament scholar G. Lohfink has vehemently denied that, on the basis of the Bible, the family and the house church can be equated.[7] As we can see from many studies in the sociology of religion on the subject of 'religion and the family', the Christian family simply has not the kerygmatic resources to fulfil the expectations embodied in the 'house church' concept. In any case it would mean a clericalising of the family, which would be resisted by even well-disposed Christians. Furthermore it would expose Christianity to the danger of privatisation by the family. It would be bound to place too great a strain on parents and to disappoint pastors. And, what is more important, expecting parents to act as catechists to their children would contradict the centuries-long process by which the Church's theology and praxis have secularised the family;[8] it would be to relieve the community, against its will, of its kerygmatic task, and to undermine its kerygmatic power. History shows us many instances of this. The locus of the kerygma is the community.

Of course, parents are very important for their children's life of faith. But we must show discretion in formulating this influence: parents facilitate the development of the emotional and psycho-social preconditions for faith; they allow them to share in their own religious practice, such as it is; they introduce their children to the community and now and again, as far as they are able, they talk to them about faith.[9] But I am convinced that they can only do this much provided the families are supported by a Christian fellowship which is both larger (and hence more public) than the family, and smaller (and hence more intimate) than the local parish community. The family's opportunities for religious education depend on there being a community fellowship which includes and transcends the family. This is attempted in basic communities for instance, but it also operates in family groups, parents' meetings, group projects, groups of friends and associations. It will be the task of pastoral care in the future to promote this kind of fellowship which roots parents and children in a larger context than the privatised family. The Church does not begin in the family. It begins in the community; the family's catechetical resources depend on it.

4. SELF-DETERMINED CHRISTIAN EXISTENCE—COMMUNITIES OF SELF-DETERMINATION

Ever since (in the limited perspective of the West) mankind has been regarded as Christian, it has been taken for granted that faith is to be handed on to 'dependents', those unable to speak for themselves. And this did not simply mean children. Adults too were seen in the same light. From the catechumenate of the ancient Church right up to the Tridentine Christian doctrine (which was still largely operative in the nineteenth century) even adults, who were the main addressees of catechesis, were dependent and immature. (Not until catechesis was built into the school system two hundred years ago was it limited to children.) And they were kept immature by a teaching of the faith which represented it one-sidedly as obedience to the Church's teaching office; what was supposed to be a 'coming of age' was in fact nothing other than further dependence. This produced a structure of proclamation which, to adults, felt like disenfranchisement: more and more they rejected and avoided it as childishness.

Those responsible in the Church simply accepted this state of affairs, and for the most part they still do, at least in old Europe. They imagine that it is enough to hand on the faith to all the children, in the family and in religion class, and then wait until they grow up. This is the way to produce a steady stream of adult Christians. In this view the faith of children is guaranteed by the 'binding obligation' of religious family education and the school religion class; the faith of adults is guaranteed by the 'binding obligation' of faith. No wonder that, in such a context, the expression 'next generation' refers exclusively to children and young people.

(a) The challenge posed by adults

From the point of view of Church history, this approach is eccentric. It was never normal in mission areas. In the future it will be important to get beyond it, however widespread it may be at present, and however much it has monopolised our practical-theological thinking and the language and procedures of pastoral praxis—e.g. those often embarrassing gestures towards children on the part of Church leaders, and the reports (including photographs!) of their especial regard for children. Without adults there can be no adult Church. The real challenge to the Church of the future is not the children but the adults.[10] The challenge which they represent may indeed be burdensome and often bring disappointment, for Christianity, 'in devoting its attention to adult catechesis, perhaps comes face to face with its own death much more explicitly than in the case of children's and young people's catechesis'.[11] But it is they who are the Church's future, if it is to have a future at all.

If the kerygma is addressed to adults, the expression 'the next generation' refers, not to the rising generation of children, but to our own generation, and in particular to the adults who largely bear responsibility within it. Nor is it a matter of faith being simply handed on to them. What happens is that, inspired by other Christians, trying to arrive at the meaning of their own lives and to work out a successful pattern of life in our society, they endeavour to verify the Gospel experience. In the process, adults are no longer the objects of catechesis: they are its subjects. This introduces an atmosphere of free and reciprocal communication within the Church. P. M. Zulehner is right when he says: 'The paramount law of human interrelationships is . . . freedom, which is by no means opposed to serious confrontation'.[12]

Thus being a Christian becomes a matter of self-determination. It becomes a sustaining element in a person's responsible life of faith with its individual features (and these features may be surprising and even disturbing in that they differ from the accepted pattern). Though remaining individual, it will not slip into an individualism which isolates itself from the Christian existence which others have attained, provided the bishops and pastors cultivate a style which invites free communication and which leaves people free even when it fails to win them over. Communication of this sort can accept (reciprocal) opposition. But it requires a tradition of striving for truth in which there is no place for silence for fear of reprisals.

(b) The possibility of choice

If the Church wants to become acquainted with self-determined adults it must offer itself as an option, it must offer a choice, in a pastoral approach which, while guarded against the purely arbitrary, is situational. In inviting people to an unbroken pattern of participation (regular Sunday worship, confession . . .) the Church is only meeting the needs of core-community Christians, i.e., those who find security in continuous contact with a community of Christians. The others, the great majority for whom being a Christian in the community is only one part of their life, are more easily attracted to special events and celebrations (birth, marriage, death, feasts, pilgrimages, holidays). Church assemblies and Catholic Congresses [*Katholikentage*] are probably so well attended precisely because they are spiritual events open to choice.

(c) Shortage of priests—an opportunity?

In the long run, self-determined Christians will only feel at home in communities which promote mutual self-determination. They need to be able to share in decision-making, and not merely in peripheral areas either. People sometimes crudely and wrongly back away from the problem of the shortage of priests and try to excuse their refusal of priestly ordination by saying that parishes without priests are able to take charge of their own community life and have the opportunity of looking after themselves. The lack of priests is neither the characteristic nor the cause of self-determination. Self-determining communities are not those which have no priest but those which elect their priest, i.e., which, if there is no other priest, select a candidate from among them and present him to the bishop for his ratification and ordination. For his part the bishop is bound to respond to their request unless there are grave reasons against it which he can make clear to everyone.

To envisage each community having a priest is not a symptom of a mistaken 'priestly centralisation'. Given the historical development, with the demands made on parishes and the many tasks they have to perform, it would be unrealistic to think that a community could go on indefinitely under honorary leadership, quite apart from the fact that it is gathered in and around the Eucharist, which is wedded to ordination. Self-determining communities live, not exclusively, yet in part, from the inspiring power of the priest. We cannot escape the shortage of priests by making it into an ideal.

Translated by Graham Harrison

Notes

1. *Catechismus Romanus, Prooemium XII.* J. Ratzinger *Die Krise der Katechese und ihre Überwindung* (Einsiedeln 1983).
2. Cf. W. Bartholomäus *Einführung in die Religionspädagogik* (Darmstadt and Munich 1983).
3. A. Teipel *Die Katechismusfrage* (Freiburg 1983) p. 369.
4. J. Ratzinger *Die Krise der Katechese* p. 27.
5. AA 11; LG 11; John Paul II *Familiaris Consortio*, 49, 51.
6. R. Graber *Die Familie als häusliches Heiligtum* (Munich 1980) p. 32.
7. G. Lohfink 'Die christliche Familie—eine Hauskirche?' in *Theologische Quartalschrift* 163 (1983) pp. 227–229,
8. See H. Tyrell 'Familie und Religion im Prozess der gesellschaftlichen Differenzierung' in *Wandel der Familie—Zukunft der Familie* ed. V. Eid and L. Vaskovics (Mainz 1982) pp. 19–74.
9. See W. Bartholomäus *Christsein lernen* (Zurich 1980).
10. See W. Bartholomäus *Einführung in die Religionspàdagogik* p. 121f., 127; *Id.* 'Gemeindekatechese' in *Theologische Quartalschrift* 162 (1982) 254–259.
11. J. Bouteiller 'Erwachsenenkatechese' in H. Schultze and H. Kirchhoff *Christliche Erziehung in Europa. IV: Frankreich* (Stuttgart and Munich 1974) p. 66.
12. P. M. Zulehner *Leutereligion* (Vienna 1982) p. 34.

PART IV

Some Particular Cases

Carlito Cenzon

Transmission of Faith in the Philippines

INTRODUCTION

THE STORY is told about the Filipinos' first contact with Christianity that Ferdinand Magellan, Portuguese navigator who sailed the oceans under the Spanish flag, upon arrival at the Philippine island of Cebu in 1521, offered the queen of that island three choices for a gift, the Rosary, the Cross, and the statue of the Santo Niño (Holy Child). The queen reportedly chose the Santo Niño and kept it among her treasures.

Later on, a basilica was built on the spot for the 'miraculous preservation of the statue'. It would become the seat of one of the principal devotions of the Filipinos.

Four hundred years afterwards, on occasion of the forthcoming visit of Pope John Paul II to the country (1981), the First Lady of the Republic of the Philippines, Mrs. Imelda Romualdez Marcos, offered to build a basilica to the Santo Niño in the archdiocese of Manila. The Archbishop of Manila, Jaime Cardinal Sin, after consultation with his senate of priests, gave the response that astounded the Catholic world—a response that said, in effect, that if this basilica be built with the money of the people, then the money could better be used to help the poor out of their misery.

This story in its two stages serves to illustrate the end-points (like the swing of the pendulum), of the story of the Filipino faith, as it is perceived today in the Philippines: one end illustrates the prevailing characteristic of the faith as one centred on devotions and temples; on the other, the gnawing and growing consciousness within the Church about the poor, who should be getting a better treatment than as mere objects of charitable acts.

Either end, and all that comes in-between (as in the pendulum), deal fundamentally with the question: What does the Filipino really think of the faith? This Filipino who received a package called Christianity, and who gradually discovers that there may be something more to the package that he received.

One may refer to a parable made famous in the Latin American Church, which reveals an ingredient in the transmission of the faith and which is applicable to the Philippine story of the faith. The parable is of the late D. T. Niles, a methodist preacher of Sri Lanka. It is referred to as the parable of the seed and the flowerpot. According to D. T. Niles, the Gospel is like a seed, which has to be sown. When sown in Palestine, a plant called Palestinian Christianity grows; sown in Rome, the plant becomes Roman Christianity. When sown in Spain, a plant called Spanish Christianity grows. Later the seed of the Gospel is brought to America, and American Christianity is born. Now the seed of the Gospel is brought to the Latin American countries. But the missionaries bring not only the seed, but also their own plant of Christianity, flowerpot included. So, he concluded, the thing to do in Latin America is to break the flowerpot, take out the seed of the Gospel, sow it in one's own cultural soil, and let one's own version of Christianity grow.

The Philippines became known to the Europeans at a not too-distant time after Latin America was colonised. And the Filipinos got the same types of missionaries: the Augustinians in 1565; the Franciscans in 1578; the Jesuits in 1581; the Dominicans in 1587, and in 1606 the Augustinian Recollects. Spaniards all, and representing so-called Post-Reformation thought, where the 'Deposit of Faith' was regulated by the Council of Trent and preserved in its 'purity' by the Spanish Inquisition. The books say that the Filipinos were practically converted by 1605. The subsequent years were one of expansion, blocked only then as now by the Filipino Muslims and Buddhists, who have not abandoned their faiths.

What has been assimilated of the Christian message and practice (seed, plant or flowerpot) is a task to which present-day Church historians, theologians, and involved Christians in the Philippines apply themselves with increasing thoroughness. The point of reference, evidently, is Vatican II, with its clarion call to *aggiornamento* and renewal.

Chesterton, the historian, once said that Christianity had not yet been tried. In the Philippine scene, Filipino Bishop Gaudencio Rosales said something with the same implications, during the International Congress on Mission held in Manila in 1979, of which he was the Director. He said that, effectively, Christ's words and deeds have not really been heard and seen among us, with the beauty that we know they possess; and that therefore a constant renewal is necessary, as individual Christians and as Christian communities.

It is in this vibrant context of search for *aggiornamento* and renewal that the transmission of the faith in the Philippines is being analysed. And since the very *basic nature* of the kind of Church-community that has grown in the Philippines is being studied, one needs to see the fundamental features in the making up of this community. A first step in this process is to see the first period of Filipino Christianity: the planting of the seed.

1. THE PLANTING OF THE SEED: ITS FEATURES

The tribe-clans of these islands who were first called 'Indios' by the Spanish navigators and later termed 'Filipinos' (after the then reigning king of Spain, Philip II) were not a homogeneous group; much less a people. Scattered in the archipelago's 7,100 islands, they spoke 78 languages.

With origins that can be traced to the peoples of South-east Asia, they carried with them their varied traditions and customs, and they possessed a religiosity. Their deities and religious beliefs and customs were interwoven with their folkways. This was the soil on which the faith was planted.

Church historians and theologians in the Philippines see certain features in this period, taken up here for our purposes. They form the basic contexts for the 'pendulum' of the story of faith in the Philippines.

First, the Filipinos who received the seed of the faith did not abandon their own gods and beliefs, in accepting the new faith. Like the queen of Cebu, they added the new faith to their treasures. This is the context on which is built the present-day challenge in the Philippine Church to look into the question of 'Folk Religiosity'. By this, analysts would infer that Filipino religiosity is simply a veneer of Catholic customs placed on animistic ones. Or, as a pagan religiosity with Catholic trappings. Or again, a skin-deep Christianity.

Second, the apparently splendid idea of the Spanish missionaries to teach the natives in their own languages did not in fact amount to more than rote memorisation of doctrines and precepts. These were not assimilated into life so as to become new principles for Christian living. It was acceptance of content without integration. Hence a split. It amounts to the same veneer of Catholicism referred to in the first case, and calls for the challenge to a synthesis between the native principles (native values) and the new ways of the faith.

Third, membership in the Church did not necessarily mean being a Christian by personal conviction. Rather, it was a 'social fact'. The thing to do was to join up, if one was to be accepted by the Spaniards and by the emerging Christian community. This would be a basis for 'membership by tradition' in the Philippines.

Fourth, the Spaniards transmitted not only their faith but also their political organisation to the Filipinos. The Spanish missionaries organised the people into towns with the satellite barrios, with the parish house as the centre of community life, and the town hall not far away. They therefore formed out of the tribes new political units. And as they were often the representatives of the Spanish government in the towns, they became the government. Faith, for the Filipino, went together with the political force of the Spanish missionary. This would eventually come to an end, with the introduction of the principle of separation of the Church and State, after the revolution against Spain (1898). The new principle, however, would not necessarily terminate the political power of the clergy. This is the background of the present-day question of 'interference' of the clergy in politics.

Fifth, the Spanish missionaries made an effort to prevent the Filipinos from being flagrantly exploited, on the principle that the natives could not be reduced to slavery by the Spaniards. As a political force, they used their position to intervene on behalf of the Filipinos. Today this question boils down to the issue of the Church's defence of human rights.

And sixth, the revolt by the Filipinos against their colonisers, which ended the period of the planting of the faith, did not take away the faith. The Filipinos did not 'throw away the gift with the rejection of the giver'. They claimed the faith for their own, and with this, the responsibility of caring for it. This is the basis for the Filipino Church Movement for self-government, some of whose members ended in schism.

2. CONSOLIDATION OF THE FAITH

The faith which survived the revolution against Spain met with new challenges for consolidation, in the wake of new developments in the Philippine scene: the arrival of the Americans, with their new ways: a new language, a new approach in government (learning the democratic way under 'American tutelage'), the public school system which brought education and English to the masses of Filipinos, together with the American values, the new and largely antagonistic Protestant sects and denominations. The period also saw the arrival of other missionaries of different nationalities and congregations, and the increase of the native clergy. All this, in the context of the newly-discovered joys of national unity and patriotism.

It will take some more time, perhaps, until we gain a full picture of what forces played most in the shaping of the Filipino of today during this second period. Conflicts were numerous and wounds ran deep, as the emerging new nation faced new options and evolved new questions. What can be pointed out as a main feature of this period for our purposes here is the following:

The *Church as a group* expands and grows to a triumphant point, in terms of organisation as an institution, and in terms of membership. There is an exultant note in references made of the Philippines as 'the only Catholic nation in Asia', with statistics placing Catholics at 85% of the population.

Put together, the Philippine Church indeed presents an impressive, colourful picture. The clergy grows, and foreign missionaries and Religious Congregations do not slacken in generosity to serve the Filipinos. The number of dioceses has grown into more than 60, with 110 bishops to govern the Church. The parishes multiplied up to 1,627 by 1981, giving an average of 31,346 inhabitants per parish, for a population of 51 million Filipinos.

Parish activities, varying in styles and dynamism, show a great mass of Catholics and an incalculable number of agents engaged in pastoral work: in devotions, worship, catechesis-education, services. Mandated organisations grow in strength and numbers and become the right-hand support of the parishes, while an increasing number of other forms of organisations, groups and movements give opportunities for creativity and deepening of expressions of faith and participation in Church life.

The religious congregations of men and women go into all kinds of apostolate to reach out to the multitudes: mission in the hinterlands, presence and service in the outskirts of towns and cities, Catholic education through the schools, the media and the arts, research and training centres, charitable institutions in the form of orphanages, asylums, hospitals, etc.

Masses of people give a colourful display of Catholic fervour in the liturgies of the churches, devotions in the form of novenas, fiestas, pilgrimages, celebrations as in Holy Week and the May festival in honour of the Blessed Mother. And training in Christian leadership is provided for the students of the Catholic schools (there are 1,624 schools listed in the Catholic Educational Association of the Philippines (CEAP) providing elementary to university education).

The separate visits of the popes to the country, Paul VI in 1970 and John Paul II in 1981, were occasions for the people to count their blessings, as both popes praised God for the Filipinos' having 'kept the faith'.

On the *political scene*, the Filipinos as an emerging nation are passing through a process of self-determination and increasing passion for the democratic way of government. The high point is the gaining of independence from the United States of America at the end of the second world war, and entrance thereby into the international world of politics as a new republic.

As a new republic, the Filipino nation in turn finds itself in the turbulent waters of nation-building, faced with the wreckage of war, coupled with the arrival into the Asian scene of a new political force, Chinese Communism.

3. THE CHURCH IN ASSESSMENT

Vatican II became a reference point for assessment in the Philippine Church. Until this moment, much of the life and orientations of the Church was left to the initiatives, inspirations (or whims) of the individual dioceses, parishes, and congregations.

Aggiornamento for the Philippine Church obviously meant looking squarely at the prevailing Philippine situation, which was being described by social analysts as one of 'social unrest'. The economy was in a poor state of affairs, with the poor (the overwhelming majority of the population) driven to a subsistence level; politics was in a mess, with graft and corruption riding high, and the stronger political leaders maintaining private 'armies'. It was a time of increasing mass demonstrations and riots. Media printed horrors of what was happening, and the phrase was born: 'the Filipinos are sitting on top of a social volcano.'

Local prophets were not wanting, among priests, sisters, laymen, the youth, in denouncing situations. The Church institution in the country was not spared. It was asked to take an attitude of renewal and change, or risk its credibility. Vatican II confirmed these prophets.

Post-Vatican II in the Philippines is still being analysed. With the inspirations of the Council as a reference point, the Filipino Church discovers itself divided into the conservative and progressive camps.

But, slowly, certain things make a headway: the creation of the Bishops' Conference of the Philippines with its Commissions; the Association of Major Religious Superiors of the Philippines (AMRSP) with its task forces. Church people get exposed to the socio-economic and political realities of the country. All kinds of groups are founded, notably the Basic Christian Communities (BCC's) with the blessing of the bishops. And as every Church group assesses itself, new initiatives sprout all over the country, in a search for a (more) meaningful Christian life, presence and service.

But in the meantime, the social realities get worse. They say that the blood of martyrs is the seed of Christianity. History will reveal who and how many of the local Christians are being the seed of the Filipino Church of tomorrow. But this last decade in the Philippines has shown a new feature for the Filipino Church. With the declaration of martial law in 1972 and the marshalling of Filipino affairs under the hands of one man, the Church enters into a novel experience: persecution on grounds of subversion, rebellion and communism. Convents, parish houses, seminaries are raided and people sent to detention. Church people suffer a taste of exile, harassment, assassination ('salvaging'). A climate of fear is created within the Church. It becomes clear that the reason for this persecution is the fact that more and more Church people make a stand against the violations of human rights.

Even as these pages are being written, there is tension in the country, as the opposition is galvanised into a united protest against the assassination of ex-Senator Benigno Aquino, as he returned from years of self-exile. The Archbishop of Manila, Jaime Cardinal Sin, called on the government to heed the cries of the people, intimating that they wait for its reply 'no longer as timid sheep, but as men and women purified and strengthened by a profound communal grief that has made them one' (Funeral Mass, 31 August, 1983).

And as the people wait, what should the Church do? This is the question. Perhaps the crucial question. And in a way, perhaps the answer is already being given: the continued defence of human rights.

To conclude as we began, our pendulum of the faith-story in the Philippines is at one end-point. What one perceives so far is that the Filipino youth is presently receiving a dosage of faith that may well define the Church of tomorrow as one committed to the shaping of this nation's destiny, based on justice.

Andreas Althammer

Handing on the Faith in the German Democratic Republic

1. THE SOCIAL CONTEXT

CHRISTIAN FAITH is handed on in the German Democratic Republic under the conditions imposed by a rigidly-led, ideologically uniform State, whose ruling party is, 'in conformity with the historical development of our times, translating into reality the aims and objectives of the working-class, as established by Marx, Engels and Lenin'.[1] Among the aims is included that of 'pursuing relentlessly the struggle against all manifestations of bourgeois ideology'.[2] Religion is one of these manifestations. For Marxism, it is of fundamental importance that religion should be overcome, since otherwise man loses himself. Religion is, according to Marx, 'the phenomenon of worldly narrowness'.[3] Human maturity is to be seen in religionlessness. It is not by chance that criticism of capitalism and criticism of religion go hand in hand. From the communist viewpoint, religion generally and Christianity in particular, are condemned to perish: religion will disappear, once its economic presuppositions have disappeared.

Nevertheless, even in the GDR, which acknowledges only *one* central ideological, Marxist-Leninist option, there are Christians, organised churches, religion, and religious worship. And, according to the Constitution, 'freedom of faith and freedom of conscience are guaranteed';[4] 'every citizen has the right to profess a religious faith, and to engage in religious activities'.[5]

These two attitudes on the subject of religion—that of the Party, which forecasts the disappearance of religion, and sees it as a relic of the past still to be overcome, and that of the State and its Constitution, which recognise religion and talk of citizens' religious rights—seem to be in tension with each other. The conflict, however, is only apparent, not real. It disappears when it is recognised that the two views are not strictly parallel. Religion is 'still' in evidence. Believers and their organisation 'still' exist.[6] While the Constitution takes into account the actual situation, the Party's statement sets out the goal. The actual situation can change; what has to be is, according to the Marxist-Leninist view, historically determined. This difference between actuality and goal conditions the way Christians feel about life. On the one hand they are satisfied with the constitutional guarantee for the Christian way of life (a guarantee which is also supported by statements from the Christian Democratic Union of the GDR, which aims to reassure Christians in the Republic, and to win over Christian fellow-citizens for the construction of socialism).

But at the same time they are very anxious about the prospects offered to them on grounds of ideology.

This anxiety becomes greater when the ideology is strongly reflected in legislative documents. Thus, for example, in the Youth Law of 1974, it says: 'An essential part of the national policy of the GDR and of the overall activity of the government, is the development of young people into socialist persons'.[7] In the School Regulation of the 29th November 1979 'the communist education of school-children' is, naturally, said to be the goal of all educational efforts in schools.[8] An oath-taking festival, with a particularly strong emotional appeal—the so-called 'Youth Dedication',[9] with its associated 'Youth-meetings'—seeks to introduce fourteen-year-olds to the socialist adult society. At the same time a uniform socialist educational system—with a ten-class technical secondary-school as its centre-piece—embraces growing children from the cradle to the university.[10] 'Free German Youth', a voluntary organisation to which, nevertheless, practically every youngster in the GDR belongs, has the task of helping 'the Party in the communist education of young people, and with their training in the Marxist-Leninist spirit'.[11] In both school and youth organisation, all educationally relevant resources are clearly controlled, from an influential and ideological point of view.

In this situation, anyone who wishes to hand on the faith must obviously regard the prediction of the historically determined end of religion as false, and must take the view that religion is part of what it means to be truly human. He thereby deviates from the ruling ideology at a fundamental point. He does not fit properly into Marxism-Leninism, even though he may accept many of its economic and social implications. Christians live in an ideologically detached way. Their situation is comparable to that of Christians who live in a country where there is a State-religion.

2. FACTS AND FIGURES

The Catholic Church in the GDR is, apart from the two compact rural Catholic areas of Eichsfeld and Sorbenland, a minority church. In former times too the Church in Middle-Germany, the birth-place of the Reformation, was a diaspora-church. It was always dependent, for both finance and personnel, on the Catholic heartland. In those earlier times, 'diaspora' denoted a situation in which Catholic Christians were scattered among Protestant Christians. Today 'diaspora' in the GDR would need to be redefined: it is the church of small numbers of believers scattered among large numbers of non-believers. Even the Evangelical Church in the GDR 'can no longer be fittingly understood or described as in any sense the Church of the people'.[12] The number of those who belong to the Catholic Church would come to about a million. It is not possible to arrive at a precise figure. The Church is divided into around 1,000 parishes and pastoral centres in six administrative districts: Erfurt-Meiningen, Magdeburg, Dresden-Meissen, (East) Berlin, Schwerin and Görlitz. In each diocese there is a catechetical board, or departments for the pastoral care of children and young people, in which materials to help and encourage the handing on of the faith are produced. A general conference of catechetical boards is responsible for the publication of catechetical books through the St Benno-Verlag in Leipzig, which is under the control of the Bishops' Conference. The dioceses have at their disposal several training-houses, where discussions with interested persons about the faith can be conducted more intensively than in the parish.

In the GDR there are some 1,100 priests, about 40 regular deacons, and approximately 600 pastoral helpers and catechists, both male and female. When priests are not available, services of worship, with preaching, are conducted in outlying places by around 700 part-time diaconal helpers. About 150 welfare workers and about 450 kindergarten teachers, who are actually part of the diaconal service of the Church, are also involved in the handing on of the faith.

3. SYNOD DECLARATIONS

Among the nine documents produced by the 'Pastoral Synod of the Catholic Church in the GDR', which met in Dresden between 1973 and 1975, is a paper on the handing on of the faith.[13] It is primarily concerned with the 'service of the Word in the liturgy; instruction; Christian witness; mutual encouragement in the faith; continuing development and spiritual discussion', and with the 'missionary task' of the Church.[14] For all kinds of proclamation, the Synod attached great importance to readiness for dialogue, which is to be understood not so much as a method, but rather as an inward attitude. Wherever the faith is handed on there must be a sympathetic regard for one's fellow human being and an understanding of his view of the world. The proclamation of the faith is not seen as the work of priests alone: 'it concerns everybody who, through baptism and confirmation, has been called to share in the responsibility for proclaiming the faith and participating in the Church's mission in the world. The whole congregation has the task of confessing, living and passing on the truth'.[15]

The document asks that, in the handing on of the faith, 'attention should be paid to priorities, and to the identification of crucial issues'. Distinctions should be made not only so far as the recipients are concerned, but also in regard to content. One very important task, almost an essential preliminary, consists in 'patiently and carefully clearing away widespread misunderstandings and distortions'.[16] Sunday preaching is seen as the 'heart of the proclamation'.[17] Proclamation strives not only to strengthen personal faith and rightly to present the basic affirmations of Christian teaching, but also 'to keep in view the environment in which the Christian lives, and to equip him to enter into dialogue with it'.[18]

The Synod would particularly like young people, who are assaulted daily by demands and offers coming at them from every side, to be taken seriously as partners in the dialogue of faith. In relation to children and young people, 'the Christian family acquires special significance as a foundation-stone of the congregation and as the area in which different generations learn to live together'.[19] Young people ought to find in the congregation a 'space of freedom' appropriate to their needs.[20] Anyone who is handing on the faith is encouraged 'to lead young people to those truths of the Gospel which contradict the spirit of the age'. In this connection the document recalls a pastoral message from the Bishops' Conference of September 1974 on the question of Christian education. In it the bishops remind the faithful, faced with ideological indoctrination, of the fact that the right of parents to decide on the religious and ideological education of their children is an established human right.[21]

For the handing on of the faith, it is not only group work that is recommended; person-to-person dialogue and the pastoral care of individuals are called for.[22] It is recognised that parents have a very important role in handing on the faith.[23] Parish councils are recommended to create a working-group for the pastoral care of children, to share in the congregation's task of leading children to faith.[24] The instruction of children should not be confined to teaching 'doctrine', but should involve the creation of experiences which establish fellowship, develop Christian conduct, and address the child in all areas of his life. It should not be forgotten 'that the environment in which the children are living is permeated with atheistic doctrine and philosophy, which set different standards, and dismiss faith as out-dated'.[25]

The Synod believes that there are special opportunities for interpreting particular life-situations in the light of faith; the sacraments, and all kinds of occasions, sacramental and otherwise, offer an invitation to show the relevance of faith to the individual or the small group in which he lives.[26] Conversations about baptism, or confession, or marriage, as well as conversations at the bedside of those who are ill, acquire a new significance. Preparation for the sacraments of penance, the eucharist and confirmation, are seen as times of special opportunity (kairos).[27] Since priests and parents are in a position to spread the faith, opportunities for further training are held to be of the greatest importance.[28] According to the Synod, a congregation has to exist for others in these ways: 'inviting, when it puts the good news of the Father's love into practice in the brotherliness of its life together; calling, when it proclaims the good news of Jesus, in season and out of season; critical, when it refuses to accept currents and opinions which are directed against the worth of the human person, but, in conformity with the Gospel, engages itself for the salvation of the world'.[29]

4. PRACTICAL STEPS[30]

(a) Parish catechesis

It can be taken for granted that in almost every parish and pastoral centre there will be the weekly catechesis. This is run under the direction of the parish, is organised in age-groups, and is led by church people. The recipients of the catechesis are school-children from the first to the tenth classes. Meetings are held on church premises and have no connection with school. Many parents of Catholic children, however, have the feeling that the catechetical teaching of the Church is simply 'religious education', carried out in a room of the presbytery. Consequently the number of children taking part in the catechesis is higher than that of children of the same age attending worship. One disadvantage resulting from the earlier pattern of religious education is the tenaciously-held idea that religious education should be left in the hands of the priest or the catechist. They are regarded as the 'proper persons' for the task, and others feel that they are excused from the bother of teaching the faith. But on the whole, parish catechesis has developed a greater openness to liturgy and prayer, to Christian service and living together, than was ever possible for the earlier pattern of religious education. Its positive characteristic is its closeness to the life of the congregation. Aids for catechetical training are published by the Benno-Verlag.[31]

(b) 'Happy hours with God'

In many parishes catechetical work is done with pre-school age children. This makes up for what ought to be done within the family. A 'mother-figure'—often a church kindergarten teacher, or a pastoral helper, in many cases an actual mother—simply tells the children stories of God. The telling of a Bible passage, or the explanation of a Church festival, is accompanied by games, singing, practical activities, introduction to Christian customs, a short prayer. 'Caritas' has worked out themes for this catechesis for younger children, and produced suitable material. Mothers who take an interest in this work often turn out in the long run to be valuable catechetical helpers.

(c) Religious 'weeks' for children[32]

Many parishes try, by means of week-long religious gatherings for children during the holidays, to help them to learn to live out together their common faith. They thus supplement and deepen the catechetical teaching given during the year, and build a bridge between the catechetical year which ends at the beginning of July and that which begins in early September. A subject of central importance for faith is spread out over six days, and broken up into six sections. Each day one particular aspect of the subject is illuminated from different sides—by means of narration, meditation, handicrafts, worship, catechetical games, pilgrimage—and often at the end there is a celebration in which the whole congregation joins. The value of these 'weeks' consists in the comprehensive insight they give into the theme, in the bringing together of learning and living, and in the relaxed, unhurried approach they permit to the essentials of the faith. In 1983 the theme for the Week was 'Reconciliation and Peace'. Each year a working-party of the catechetical boards produces a hand-book containing catechetical material, services of worship, songs, and suggestions for other activities.

(d) Religious 'weeks' for young people

The success and catechetical value of the children's 'week' led in different parishes to a demand for a similar week for young people—especially for girls and boys in the ninth and tenth classes. The handbook for 1983 proposed some ethical reflections: Can we live with lies? Can we think only of today? Should we live and let live? Can we think only of ourselves? It took up the theme of the bishops' pastoral message for Lent. The individual themes are interchangeable. The undertaking does not yet have the character of a catechetical course.

(e) Congregational catechesis

If 'congregational catechesis' means catechesis in church as opposed to catechesis in school, then we have nothing but congregational catechesis in the GDR. But if the expression means that lay people are accepting responsibility for handing on the faith, and are making themselves available, with their ideas and their testimony, then the Church in the GDR is only at the very beginning of such an enterprise. Here and there, mothers become involved with children preparing for their first communion. In many places, adults help with preparation for confirmation, by allowing themselves to be enlisted as leaders of confirmation groups. Where a child is growing up a long way from the presbytery, the priest will often ask a believer to undertake the child's first introduction to the faith. But in spite of these things we cannot speak of a break-through to a new concept of catechesis. The question needs also to be asked whether, in the situation existing in the GDR, the new approach ought in all cases to replace the present one.

(f) Catechetical hospitality

A catechetical method adapted to the needs of a scattered community has been practised for many years in the parish of Waren.[33] The catechist does not go to visit the children and young people in the seventy-two villages which belong to the parish; instead they come to a catechetical week-end in the main town. Families offer hospitality to the children, and many helpers organise the week-end's instruction and attend to the transport problems. Here the handing on of the faith has really and truly become the concern of the whole congregation, which is now the 'doer of the catechesis'. The work of instruction can thus be happily linked with the gathering together of the scattered members of the community.

5. PROBLEMS

(a) The role of the family

The handing on of the faith in the GDR is, basically, family-orientated. The hope is that in Christian families, linked up with the Church, the children will grow up to be Christians linked up with the Church, and that in this way the Church will go on reproducing itself. But unfortunately there are ever fewer Christian marriages. Mixed marriages, including those with atheists, have now become the rule, and fully Catholic marriages the exception. In the long run, the handing on of the faith can not be achieved simply by the Church reproducing itself internally. The Catholic Church in the GDR needs a system of religious education for children and young people from homes where the parents no longer believe, just as it is in need overall of a powerful missionary impulse towards members of the new society. For the most part, the Church offers faith to those who are outside it by appealing to the baptism which they underwent as infants. Faith is thus offered as a sort of 'second delivery'. The Church simply does not know how to take its message to interested people who have no connection with it. To do this would involve a complete change of approach.

(b) Need for a Christian sub-culture

A Christian culture affecting people's life-style is in the process of disappearing in the GDR. Nor can the Evangelical Church hope to reactivate it. But we could strive for a Christian 'sub-culture', a Catholic community-life in small groups which would extend beyond the limits of our modern nuclear family. The development of this kind of small Christian living-space cannot be on a narrowly Catholic basis, as in the nineteenth century, but will require openness—ecumenical and otherwise. The ideal of believers living as a family, for which we have often striven, could be realised in this way. The missionary principle of Clement of Alexandria, according to which anyone who has lived in a Christian family for a year becomes a Christian, could thus be put to the test, and its relevance shown for the handing on of the faith in the GDR.[34]

(c) Catechetical methods and the social relevance of faith

The handing on of the faith, or rather the frequent failure to hand it on, is a matter of serious concern to pastors and catechists. They feel that their catechetical work is ineffective. In many places the attempt has been made to arrest this tendency to failure by the use of new methods, by means of a wholly anthropologically-based catechesis, or by substituting 'teaching by objectives' for the more normal simple plan of instruction. Of course teaching methods could be greatly improved, but the significance of catechesis depends only secondarily upon method. Its primary significance has to do with the relevance of faith and of the Church in society as a whole. If this disappears, then catechesis will go along with it. It is unfair to hold those who are professionally charged with the handing on of the faith responsible for this situation.

(d) Warning against hasty comparisons

The experiences and problems connected with the handing on of the faith in the GDR are not typical for all Eastern-European countries governed by Marxist-Leninist parties. The constitutional separation of State and Church allows the Church in the GDR a certain independence in relation to the Constitution. The gap between the constitutional recognition of what is, and the party-ideological conception of the goal to be attained, varies in width from country to country. In the GDR the two are not so close together as to leave no room for movement. Moreover there are different traditions in different countries. The role played by religion in society in the past, and the nearness of the Church to ordinary people, vary from country to country. It is not, therefore, possible to give an account of the handing on of the faith in all countries where socialism is a 'reality' by treating one particular country as a typical example.

Translated by G. W. S. Knowles

Notes

1. Statute of the Socialist Unity Party of Germany. Preamble. 3rd ed. (Berlin 1976) 5.
2. *Ibid.* 7.
3. Karl Marx *Zur Judenfrage* (1843) MEW 1,352.
4. Constitution of the GDR, Art. 20.
5. *Ibid.* Art. 39,1.
6. Communist writers sometimes take the view that the phenomenon of religion may prove more persistent than was at first expected. Olof Klohr 'Tendenzen des Absterbens von Religion und Kirche in der DDR' in *Voprosy filosofii* (1973/4) pp. 147–154.
7. Youth Law of the GDR, of the 28th February 1974, para. 2,1 (Berlin—Staatsverlag der DDR—1974) 12.
8. Regulation on the establishment of a set pattern for comprehensive polytechnic secondary schools—School Regulation—of the 29th November 1979, para. 3,3; 21,3; and see 29,1. According to para. 35,1 parents have also a 'responsibility for the all-round education and the communist training of children and young people' (*Gesetzblatt 1*, no. 44, pp. 433ff.).
9. Academy of Pedagogical Sciences in the GDR *Das Bildungswesen der Deutschen Demokratischen Republik* 2nd ed. (Berlin 1983) pp. 71f.; Central Committee for the Service of Youth in the GDR *Handbuch zur Jugendweihe* (Berlin 1974); *Jugendweihe. Zeitschrift für Mitarbeiter und Helfer*, published by the Central Committee for the Service of Youth in the GDR (Berlin). 8 issues annually; K. Richter 'Rites and Symbols in an Industrial Culture as Illustrated by their Use in a Socialist Context' in *Concilium* 102 (1977) pp. 72–82; A. Althammer 'Jugendweihe und Pastoral' in *Internationale Katholische Zeitschrift* 11 (1982) pp. 573–593.
10. *Das Bildungswesen in der DDR* pp. 17–25.
11. Statute of the Socialist Unity Party of Germany, no. 65.
12. Karl Heinrich Bieritz 'Der Öffentlichkeitsanspruch des Gottesdienstes in einer Nicht-mehr-Volkskirche' in *Pastoraltheologische Informationen* 1/1981 p. 38.
13. Resolution of the Pastoral Synod: 'Aspekte des Verkündigungsdienstes der Gemeinde' (Leipzig—St Benno-Verlag—1976).
14. *Ibid.* no. 1.
15. *Ibid.* no. 9.
16. *Ibid.* no. 16.
17. *Ibid.* no. 22.
18. *Ibid.* no. 18.
19. *Ibid.* no. 28.
20. *Ibid.* no. 29.
21. *Ibid.* no. 32.
22. *Ibid.* no. 38f.
23. *Ibid.* no. 45.
24. *Ibid.* no. 49 and 57.
25. *Ibid.* no. 54.
26. *Ibid.* no. 61f.
27. *Ibid.* no. 64 (E 16) and 65.
28. *Ibid.* no. 73; 77; 78–82.
29. *Ibid.* no. 86.
30. See F. G. Friemel 'Bericht über einige katechetische Aktivitäten in den katholischen Bistümern in der DDR' in *Die Christenlehre* 29 (1976) pp. 169–175.
31. The books for the lower age-range are: *Kinder Gottes* (Children of God), *Zeichen der Liebe* (Signs of Love), and *Gotteswort* (God's Word); for 'Faith and Life' teaching in the more senior groups a revised form of *Grundriss des Glaubens* (Outline of Faith) is appearing in 1984; for young people in the 9th and 10th years *Glaube aktuell* (Faith Today) is used.

32. Josefa Kendzia 'Religiöse Kinderwochen' in *Neue Wege für Religionsunterricht und Katechese* ed. Wolfgang Nastainczyk (Würzburg 1974) pp. 74–80.

33. Ludwig Schöpfer 'Religiöse Unterweisung in einer katholischen Diasporagemeinde' in *Die Christenlehre* 29 (1976) pp. 175ff.; Georg Handy 'Eine Gemeinde stellt sich vor' in *Tag des Herrn* 30 (1873) pp. 148ff.

34. See Franz Georg Friemel 'Gemeinde—Hilfe zum Glauben' in *Sperare. Pastorale Aufsätze* ed. Hugo Aufderbeck (Leipzig 1979) pp. 170–183.

Virgil Elizondo

Transmission of the Faith in the USA

TO WRITE about the transmission of faith to the next generation in the USA is both a very complex and a very challenging task. It is a country of very large proportions and very diverse peoples. It is divided by four time zones and expands from the Atlantic Ocean to the Pacific Ocean including the Hawaiian Islands. Although the dominant cultural patterns are white, Anglo-Saxon and Protestant, it is still a nation of nations—a population made up of many immigrant groups. Ancient pre-Colombian inhabitants, commonly yet erroneously called 'Indians', co-exist with descendants of the early colonists, with Africans who were brought in as slaves and with the many waves of immigrant that have come from all the nations of the world.

The diversity of peoples which make up the USA is only surpassed by the many varieties of Christian denominations, each with various diverse cultural expressions of that denomination. It is not uncommon to hear about the Irish Dominicans, the German Benedictines, the Polish Franciscans, the Italian Salesians, the Mexican Baptists, or the African Methodists. National seminaries, parishes and religious congregations were the rule of the day until recent times and some still continue. As new waves of immigrants come in to the country, new national communities are once again needed and flourishing.

The people of the United States are very religious and the great presence of many churches is evident to new immigrants and tourists. Yet Americans feel quite free to go from one denomination to another. It has been said that the United States is so religious that it creates a new religion each day! This gives rise to what is commonly called: 'Jesus, cafeterial style'—you can walk along the street and go to the Catholic Christ, to the Methodist one, to the Baptist one, to the Congregational one, to the Free One, so on *ad infinitum*. You have the choice of Christ as you like it as you have the choice of many foods in a cafeteria as you like them. The predominant religion in the United States is certainly a Christian religion, yet its many and increasing varieties make it appear more as a Christian Babel than a Christian Pentecost.

To a certain degree, faith is being transmitted through the traditional sources: the experience of faith in the believing and practising family, the Catholic schools, religious education programmes, Sunday School for the Protestants, radio and television and personal revival activities, and the general activity of the parishes. There are certainly some very active and dynamic parishes in the United States through which the faith is being transmitted to many people. Furthermore, Christian family movements are instilling Christian principles and ideals in their children through a variety of faith experiences that are truly admirable. The new catechetical series being put out by the major publishers of the US are excellent introductions into the life of faith of many youngsters.

Yet, in moving around the USA and especially outside of the normal domain of the Church, I am convinced that truly conversion experiences followed by a life of Christian discipleship is taking place more commonly through non-church situations. It is this growing phenomena that we'll try to explore in this brief article.

1. THE MOVEMENTS FOR JUSTICE

For many young people in the 1960s, the primary conversion experience and call to discipleship came through their participation in the civil rights movements—especially those inspired and led by Dr Martin Luther King. They were religious crusades for liberty and justice—the liberty and justice of the Kingdom. Movements such as Sojourners, the Catholic Worker Movement, the Farm Worker Movement, Pax Christi, and others, did not call for violence but they refused to conform themselves to the situations of institutional violence of long standing in this country. Peace based upon justice had to be worked and sacrificed for. It would not happen automatically.

Religious chants and prayers animated the struggles and marches to the racist cities and countryside of the United States. In the name of the God of the Exodus who liberated the people from enslavement and in the name of the God of Jesus, who out of death had brought life, many joined together to fight against the persons and structures that enslaved people and denied life to the Blacks, the 'Indians', and Hispanics! God was being met and experienced not in theory or in concepts, not in seminaries or cathedrals, not in worship or religious education programmes, but in the concrete praxis of the struggle for the liberation of all the oppressed. Religious bigots quickly labeled these crusaders as Communists and rabble-rousers! As with early Christianity, many religious people of that time saw these Biblically prophetic movements as unauthorised groups of trouble-makers. They had come to disturb the 'law and order' and the 'peace' of a society in which law and order had served to legitimise and hide the ongoing violence and destructiveness of the institutions.

Many of those who participated in the movements were repulsed and disgusted with the hypocrisy of organised religion and the emptiness of their theological and doctrinal discourse. Religion in America had sacralised and legitimised racism and injustice. Yet, come Sunday morning and millions of people would go to the churches to thank God for their goodness and their purity. Hypocrisy of the worst kind seemed to be the under-pin of the institutional religions of the USA. In the movements, the participants experienced fellowship, concern and commitment. Most of all they experienced the pain and joy of a life that was truly worth dying for. Neither harrassment, jail, ridicule nor even death, could hamper the spirit of the movements. 'We shall overcome' became the kerygma of the new movement. Its enthusiasm and total commitment attracted thousands and new names were added to their ranks each day.

Participants in the movement relativised many of the old dogmas and religious stereotypes of each other. They simply were not even brought up or discussed. They did not matter. In the struggle we all experienced a new unity which far transcended any of the old divisions. Rich and poor, young and old, clergy, religious and laity, Black, white and brown, educated and illiterate, Catholic, Baptists and others, all participated equally as children of the God of life. In many ways this was the beginning of a truly post-Reformation united Christian experience. We prayed and joined in common faith celebrations. A new ecclesial unity was experienced which transcended all the previous doctrinal divisions. It was in the movements that Christ and the God that He had introduced us to came to life in us. We experienced the dynamism of the Spirit as it was experienced in early Christianity of Acts which pierced through all the cultural, racial and religious divisions to bring about a new community of humanity. The movement itself provided the primary encounter with the crucified-risen Lord as the Lord of liberty and life. It was in the daily struggle for equality (Civil Rights Movement, United Farm Workers, Chicano Movement, Native American Movement for Peace, Pax Christi, Anti-War Movements during Vietnam) and freedom from the demands of the materialist society (the Hippies. . . .) that people discovered a new faith. These movements were animated by Biblical evangelicals, Life Sojourners, which gave the people a scriptural and theological base for their new experience of God in the context of a contemporary Exodus movements for life.

2. THE EXPERIENCE OF PERSONAL GOD

These experiences led to a new God-imagery which was to have profound and multiple effects in the entire catechetical movement in the USA. From the God as stern judge and lawgiver who would punish the sinner with everlasting damnation in hell, we moved to the God of Exodus who hears the cries of His people, sees their affliction and wills to save them; to the God of the exile who remains with His people in their suffering in foreign lands; to the God of Jesus who is the all-loving Father whose mercy knows no limits and who will liberate his people even from the bondage of death.

This God came alive and is present in the person of Jesus. It is in Jesus that we meet the living God. Thus the rise of the various Jesus-movements. People did not just want to learn about God, they wanted to meet the person of Jesus! (This startled and shocked many biblical experts who were moving more and more away from Jesus and simply into the meaning of the text of the Scriptures.) People wanted to experience His presence, to hear His words, to feel His rehabilitating and healing grace and to enjoy His compassion and forgiveness. From a doctrinal knowledge of the Second Person of the Blessed Trinity who was made man for our salvation we pass to the Son of the All-loving Father who in the Spirit makes us His brothers and sisters and children of the same Father. In Him we receive through the Spirit the very same life. The quest to meet Jesus of my life continues to be a source of conversion and discipleship among many of the young people of all walks of life and of all denominations in the United States.

But much more than the shift in God-imagery was the change in the pedagogical approach itself. Whereas in the past much of the faith had been transmitted through concepts and rules (doctrine and church law), today the role of experience is accepted as primary in the transmission of faith both among the younger generation and among the majority of today's teachers. The Lord must be experienced before He can be studied. They are not so much interested in philosophical-theological expositions or even doctrines as they are in the continuity of core experiences of loving, caring and forgiving. It is from within these experiences that we can reflect critically the meaning of our faith. It is from within the experience of the Christian movement itself that we begin to search the meaning of this movement. This calls for new approaches to both theologising and catechetising. From religious education classes we have passed to a multiplicity of 'happenings' wherein faith can be experienced. It is from within the context of this life-giving faith experiences that Christian educators reflect with their students the meaning of faith.

For many, the confessional and institutional make-up of Churches (Catholic or other) is quite secondary to the experience of fellowship, commitment and celebration. This has led people to radically change their lifestyle—from the individualistic highly competitive and materialistic ideal of the USA to a communitarian model based on prayer, simplicity and sharing.

They are not as much concerned with assent or denial of doctrine as they are with togetherness—they want to touch and feel God's love in the person of those around—in the person of the lonely and the needy. God's presence is truly felt and experienced in the communitarian encounter. The younger generation does not want simply to experience but neither do they want to have doctrine forced upon them. They have questions about the real issues of life; about social enslavement and blindness, about values and priorities, about personhood and family; about sex and its role in a community of love; and they certainly have questions about death and the hereafter. They equally have questions about peace and the task of peacemaking; about hunger in the world; about blatant injustice in large portions of our planet; about the efforts of the nations of the world to destroy each other through instruments of war. They want an experience of fellowship but they certainly do not want to remain there—they seek transcendence and ultimate meaning all the more.

3. DISCIPLESHIP

For many these core experiences coupled with critical reflection about the meaning of faith in today's world has led them to volunteer to work for one year, two, three or more years in the poorest areas of our own country and in foreign countries. Many have gone as volunteers and many of the traditional religious communities are organising affiliates who will dedicate a certain number of years of their life to work amongst the poor. Our youth does not want an easy Christianity and many are committing themselves in truly heroic ways but they are not committing themselves to institutional models such as priests, brothers or sisters. Too many of them see these roles simply as bureaucratic functions and not truly as models of Christian discipleship. I would dare say that I suspect that a new form of religious life is already beginning to emerge amongst many of the young men and women who have returned from this experience of voluntary service to live a stable life in a community creating a family and children. They continue to meet together in groups of prayer, of service and of fellowship. Through them the faith is certainly being transmitted in a new way. Yet this new way experiences growing frustrations with the on-going activity of a clergy-dominated Church.

4. FROM THE EXPERIENCE OF POWERLESSNESS

There is still another fascinating shift that is transferring the transmission of faith from the organised churches to the periphery of Church and society. With the growing demands which a technical, very materialistic and highly competitive society places upon persons to succeed, the use of alcohol and drugs continues to grow in alarming proportions. More and more become rejects of society because they become alcoholics or drug addicts. When they hit rock-bottom, some finally turn for help—to Alcoholics Anonymous or to Narcotics Anonymous. (Others, the more unfortunate ones, simply continue in their sickness to live a life of death in society.) The God 'of power and might' who seems to have abandoned them is now replaced by the God of infinite love and mercy who seeks us out in our weaknesses. The old conversion experience of Augustine becomes more and more of a role model for many alcoholics and drug addicts of today. As one priest who went through such an experience told me, 'The refuse of society have introduced me to the person of God. What the best theologians and spiritual guides had not succeeded in doing for me, the ridiculed and rejected of the world have accomplished. They have taught me how to visit with God, how to pray, how to trust. With them I have met the living God.' Paul's statement: 'My grace is enough for you, for in your weakness power reaches perfection . . . for when I am powerless, it is then that I am strong' (2 Cor. 12:9–10), takes on more and

H

more importance in our times. For a society that is geared towards competition and winning and that easily deifies those who make it to the top, the millions who do not make it are doomed to rejection, social pressures, guilt feelings, shame and a deep sense of unworthiness. In such a society, it becomes impossible, even in the best of churches, to truly meet the God of Jesus since we tend to worship more naturally Prometheus masked as the Christian God than the God of the weak and the powerless who presents himself to us throughout the pages of the scriptures.

It is amazing how today in Japan more converts to Christianity are being made through Alcoholics Anonymous and Narcotics Anonymous than by all the previous efforts of the missionaries. For highly competitive people, like those of the United States, a God of power and success meant little to nothing, but the God who reaches out to us in our utter and complete powerlessness has truly appealed to them as the living God who can rescue them from their suicidal dilemma, save them from death and liberate them into new life. It is this God of powerlessness that is converting the proud and power-seeking Japanese.

Because organised religion has been on the side of power, it has tended to present a God of power who blesses only the powerful curses the weak and condemns them as sinful. For growing numbers of people, this is not the God who saves but rather the God who unmercifully crushes. In the experience of Alcoholics Anonymous or Narcotics Anonymous, people who have failed not because of their own fault but because of the incredible pressures from society experience a unique resurrection and call to life. The very recognition of their own powerlessness, and seeing and hearing personal testimonies from many people like themselves about God's unlimited love, mercy and power have totally rehabilitated them, they personally experience God's unquestioned love and acceptance. In admitting their powerlessness in a society which canonises and demands power, people are able to allow in and discover the one power that truly counts—the power of God unto wholeness. In this experience of the power of the Gospel—not a power to control but a power that truly brings strength out of weakness and life out of death, those who have been living a type of death in society now come to life. For many young people who at an early age already experience this total abandonment and rejection due to the unlimited pressures of society, Alcoholics Anonymous and Narcotics Anonymous have functioned for them as a primary Church experience in their lives. It is here that they meet the living God, convert, throw away their crutches of alcohol or drugs and truly get up and walk erect as full men and women who are now free, free in the power of God to accept themselves as they are without competing with others or feeling inferior to others but truly celebrating what they are, the images of God called to give whatever they have to bettering society. It is amazing the depth of faith of the people who have gone through this religious experience. It cuts through all walks of life as rich and powerful, highly educated and illiterate, ordinary housewives or husbands, religious and atheists, come to meet a living God precisely at the moment of their absolute powerlessness.

5. FUNDAMENTALISM

Finally, there is another source of transmission of faith that is rapidly growing in this country: fundamentalism. As the credibility gap of both Church and society continues to increase and people are bombarded with more and more information, the need for ultimate security and certitude seems to grow more and more. Hence, people—young and old, of all ethnic groups and educational levels—are turning to biblical fundamentalism: 'It's in the Bible.' It's a simplistic, non-critical reading of the Bible which nevertheless is quite appealing and satisfying to growing numbers of people both within the Catholic and Protestant traditions. They seem to respond to the needs of people to have simple and clearcut answers. These movements tend to be very moralistic, highly emotional, and very demanding of their members. Yet in a highly permissive society wherein there are many opinions about everything, this type of simple fundamentalism seems to respond to the need of people for ultimate and clearcut security. They call forth an immediate religious experience and demand no thinking on the part of the followers. Just follow the simple and clearcut dictates of the Bible and you will be saved.

6. CONCLUDING REMARKS

There is a great religious revival in the United States. The people who go to churches are on the increase as are also the number of churches. Just what this religious and Church experience means and how it relates to the biblical faith of the scriptures would take another issue to explore.

But the transmission of deep faith to the next generation, versus the simple sensation or experience of religion in a revival tent or Catholic liturgy is taking place much more through unsuspected movements and events than through the institutional and well-organised programmes of the Church. Whereas this might appear alarming to some who would like to continue being in charge and in control of the workings of the spirit of God, it is quite fascinating and refreshing to me. For it seems to me in studying the transmission of faith through the pages of the Bible and its rich history, that God always works through unsuspected persons, movements and situations, and in totally unimagined places. When and where we least expect, God's liberting and saving grace irrupts. There will certainly be new expressions of the one true faith which will emerge in years to come. I do not foresee that the churches will disappear, but I certainly see that the Christians of the next generations will relate to the Church institutions in quite different ways than we have in the past. The faith will continue to be transmitted, the concrete form and shape that the faith community will take is something that will emerge in the days to come.

Contributors

ANDREAS ALTHAMMER is a pseudonym. The author's identity is known to the editorial board.

WOLFGANG BARTHOLOMÄUS was born in 1934 in Osnabruck. He studied philosophy and theology in Frankfurt-am-Main G, the pedagogy of religion and the sciences of communication in Munich and depth-psychology in Vienna. Since 1972 he has been Professor of Religious Education and Kerygmatics in the Faculty of Catholic Theology of the University of Tübingen. His publications include: *Evangelium als Information. Elemente einer theologischen Kommunikationstheorie* (1972); *Kleine Predigtlehre* (1974); co-author with A. Stock of *Wissenschaftstheorie und Studienreform* (1975); *Religionsunterricht im Spannungsfeld von Kirche und Theologie* (1976); *Christsein lernen* (1981); *Einführung in die Religionspädagogik* (1983).

OSCAR BEOZZO was born in 1941 and ordained priest in 1964. He did philosophical studies at São Paulo, theology at the Gregorian University, Rome, and sociology and social communications at Louvain, Belgium. He is secretary of the CESEP (Ecumenical Centre of Service for Evangelisation and Popular Education) and professor in the Faculty of Theology of São Paulo. He has written articles for the *Revista Eclesiástica Brasileira* and *Vozes*, collaborated in vol. II/2 of the *Historia da Igreja na América Latina* (1980), *Materliales para una Historia de la Teologia en A.L.* (1981) and author of the book *Leis e Regimentos de Missao—A Política Indigenista no Brasil* (1983). He is the co-ordinator for Brazil of CEHILA (Comissão de Estudos de História da Igreja na América Latina).

GOTTFRIED BITTER, CSSp, was born in 1936 in Wevelinghoven in the Rhineland. In 1957 he joined the Holy Ghost Fathers, continuing his studies in theology, philosophy, art and music at the universities of Freiburg and Münster. In 1975 he became lecturer for religious education at Würzburg University, in 1977 professor for religious education and catechetics at the University of Bochum, and in 1980 professor for religious education and homiletics at the University of Bonn. As well as having published a number of religious books and commentaries, he has written articles on the conditions governing an understanding and communication of the Christian faith in the context of religious education and homiletics. His books include *Erlösung* (1976); together with G. Miller (ed.), *Konturen heutiger Theologie* (1976); with A. Exeler *et al.*, *Grundriß des Glaubens, Katholischer Katechismus* (1980; with English, French and Polish translations); *Das Leben wagen* (1982); with N. Mette (ed.), *Leben mit Psalmen, Entdeckungen und Vermittlungen* (1983).

CARLITO CENZON, CICM, was born in Baguio City, the Philippines, in 1939. Ordained priest in 1965, he studied history at St Louis University, Baguio City, the University of Santo Tomas, Manila, and the Ateneo de Manila University. Between 1966–1968 he was assistant priest at the Natonin Mission in the Mountain Province of the Philippines. From 1970–1971 he was rector of CICM Minor Seminary in Bacolod, Philippines. Between 1972–1982 he did mission work in Brazil, and since 1983 he has been Vice-provincial for the CICM RP Province. He has written articles for reflection and animation, in magazines and newsletters of the congregation, for internal use.

VIRGIL ELIZONDO, PhD, STD was born in San Antonio, Texas (USA), studied at the Ateneo University (Manila), at the East Asian Pastoral Institute (Manila), and at the Institut Catholique (Paris). Since 1971, he has been president of the Mexican American Cultural Center in San Antonio. He has published numerous books and articles and has been on the editorial board of of *Catequesis Latino Americana* and of the *God With Us Catechetical Series*, Sadlier Publishers, Inc. (USA), and is on the editorial board of *Concilium*. He does much theologial reflection with the grass-roots people in the poor neighbourhoods of the USA.

CASIANO FLORISTÁN was born in 1926 at Arguedas (Spain). He studied chemistry at Zaragoza, philosophy at Salamanca and theology at Innsbruck, and was ordained priest in 1956. He was awarded a Doctorate in 1959 at Tübingen. Since 1960 he has been a teaching professor of the Pontifical University of Salamanca at the Department of Pastoral Studies in Madrid. He was Principal of the Instituto Superior de Pastoral in Madrid from 1963–1973. He teaches summer courses in several South American countries. His publications include *La vertiente pastoral de la sociología religiosa* (1960), *La parroquia, comunidad eucarística* (1961), *El año litúrgico* (1962), *Teología de la acción pastoral* (1968), *El Catecumenado* (1972) and *La evangelización, tarea del cristiano* (1978).

JAMES W. FOWLER serves as professor of theology and human development and director of the Center for Faith Development at Candler School of Theology of Emory University. Professor Fowler, a United Methodist minister, received his doctorate in religion and society from Harvard University in 1971. His books include *To See the Kingdom: The Theological Vision of H. Richard Niebuhr* (1974), *Stages of Faith* (1981), and *Becoming Adult, Becoming Christian* (1984). He is co-author or editor of *Life-Maps: Conversations on the Journey of Faith* (1978), *Trajectories in Faith* (1980), and *Toward Moral and Religious Maturity* (1980).

ANDRÉ GODIN, SJ, is a member of the Société Belge de Psychanalyse and has lectured on the psychology of religion in Rome, Brussels (Centre 'Lumen Vitae' until 1975) and Charleroi, and as guest professor at Laval University (Quebec) and the Gregorian University (Rome). He is Secretary of the Commission internationale de psychologie religieuse scientifique (Luxemburg). Recent publications include: *The Psychology of Religious Vocations: Problems of the Religious Life* (1983) and *The Psychology of Religious Experiences* (1983).

NORBERT METTE, born in 1946 in Barkhausen/Porta, studied theology and social sciences and gained his doctorate in theology. He is a *Privatdozent* in the Catholic faculty of theology at Münster and teaches practical theology at Paderborn. He is married with three children. Among his most recent contributions in the fields of pastoral theology and religious education are *Voraussetzungen christlicher Elementarerziehung*, (1983), and, jointly with H. Steinkamp, *Sozialwissenschaften und Praktische Theologie* (1983).

JOHANNES (HANS) VAN DER VEN was born in 1940 in Breda in the Netherlands. He studied theology at the diocesan seminary at Breda and in the Theological Faculty at Nijmegen University, qualifying as a doctor in pastoral theology in 1973. From 1968 onwards, he was an assistant lecturer, from 1976 a lecturer and from 1980 has been professor of pastoral theology, with special emphasis on catechetics, in the Theological Faculty of the Catholic University of Nijmegen. He is the leader of a research programme entitled 'The Evaluation of Pastoral Activity', which incorporates several research projects and is characterised by an empirical theological approach. His publications include: *Katechetische Leerplanontwikkeling* (1973); *Graven naar geloof* (1976), in collaboration with W. J. Berger, and *Kritische godsdienstdidactiek* (1982). He has also written many articles, including 'Op weg naar een empirische theologie' in *Meedenken met Edward Schillebeeckx* (1983).

GERARD VOGELEISEN was born in 1929 in Colmar, France. After ordination as a priest in 1954, he served as a curate and school chaplain. He gained a post-graduate degree in psychology and a doctorate in theology, and is now professor in the faculty of Catholic theology at Strasbourg. Since 1970 he has been director of the Institute of Religious Education there. He also works in psycho-sociology, educational theory and adult education. He has written several articles, especially in *Catéchèse*, *Katechetische Blätter* and *Religions-pädagogische Beiträge*. He is also co-author of a history of religious education in France between 1893–1980 (1981).

JOHN HENRY WESTERHOFF III was born in Paterson, New Jersey (USA) in 1933. He is a priest of the Episcopal Church. After the completion of his theological studies at Harvard University he served for eight years as a parish priest. Later he completed doctoral graduate studies in the history and philosophy of education at Columbia University. Since 1974 he has been professor of practical theology at the divinity school in Duke University and serves as editor of the journal *Religious Education*. Among his numerous works are *Will Our Children Have Faith?* (In Japanese and Spanish), *Liturgy and Education Through the Life Cycle* (with W. Willimon), *Generation to Generation* (with G. K. Neville), *The Spiritual Life: Learning East and West* (with J. Eusden), *A Faithful Church: Issues in History of Catechesis* (ed.), *Christian Believing* (with U. Holmes), *Who Are We: A Quest for a Religious Education* (ed.), *Bringing Up Children in the Christian Faith, Building God's People in a Materialistic Age*, and *A Pilgrim People: Learning Through Church Year*.

Concilium statement on liberation theology

Issued at the Annual General Meeting held at Berg en Dal,
near Nijmegen, Netherlands, June 1984

LIBERATION theology is in the public eye. It has been the subject of comment by high
ecclesiastical authorities, of articles in various newspapers and reviews, and of questions
put to several individual theologians. We consider it our duty to take a position on this
problem.

(1) *Birth of basic Christian communities and of the theology of liberation.* Since Vatican
II, we have witnessed a real renewal in the life of the churches in poor countries. This has
shown itself in the flourishing of numerous basic ecclesial communities and of groups of
biblical reflection, in a new vitality of faith among the people, and in the involvement of
Christians (laity, priests and bishops) in the struggle for the defence of the right of the
poorest to life.

In this way, the Church has begun to enter the world of the poor and to share their
destiny, while at the same time the people have assumed new responsibilities within its
communion. From the moment that the People of God committed itself to this road, there
began a critical reflection whose purpose has been to address the problem of the oppressed
in the light of the faith and to promote their full liberation.

Simultaneously, in other contexts but as part of the same vital movement, there has
been a process of liberation and reflection among women, finding themselves marginal to
the life of society and of the Church, and among races and cultures conscious of their
position as minorities in Church and society.

(2) *Current tensions.* These developments, and the hopes and claims which they
embody, have provoked contrary reactions, incomprehension and even hostility on the
part of those who hold political and economic power. We have seen men and women
disappear, forced into exile, tortured and assassinated. These things are absolutely
unacceptable. Within the Church, while some holding positions of authority have
sometimes supported and accepted these movements of liberation, we have also seen
people defamed, forbidden to teach theology, rendered suspect of infidelity to the
Christian message, and accused of substituting ideologies for the Gospel, under the
influence of Marxism. Against such procedures we register a strong and vigorous protest.

These are tensions necessary to the life of the Church, but today these are exacerbated
by integrist and neoconservative groups. Resisting all social change and holding that
religion has nothing to do with politics, they fight against movements of liberation and
make choices that constitute an offence against the poor and oppressed.

All of these factors have created a climate which is unfavourable to the search for new ways of being church and of proclaiming the Gospel.

(3) *The position of the theologians of 'Concilium'.* Wishing to remain always faithful to the orientations and inspirations of Vatican II, in line with a preferential option for the poor, and in keeping with its own distinctive theological identity, *Concilium* expresses its solidarity with these new movements, with the local churches affected by them, and with the theologians of liberation, both within the Catholic Church and in other Christian churches. We, the theologians of *Concilium*, wish to express our solidarity not only with their theological thought but also with the concrete positions that they take.

In doing this, we are pursuing an orientation taken within recent years, as evidenced by the creation of new sections (Third World Theology, Feminist Theology) and by the line taken in several recent numbers of the review. A future number of *Concilium* will be devoted to the ecclesial context within which these tensions have to be situated.

Certainly, it is not our pretension to possess the fullness of truth, and we are conscious of being but one voice among several, a voice, however, that is fully ecclesial. In fact, it is a sign of the fecundity of the Gospel today that it is lived in different contexts and in different ways. Theology is but an expression of, and a reflection upon, this situation, a situation that is cause for joy and not for alarm. This is the dimension of pluralism inherent to catholicity. To fulfil its role, theology needs that freedom of research and expression which we claimed for it in our declaration of 1971.

(4) *Conclusion.* As these movements are a sign of hope for the whole Church, any premature intervention from higher authorities risks stifling the Spirit, which animates and guides local churches. We express our strong solidarity with these movements of liberation and with their theology. We protest against the suspicions and unjust criticisms registered against them. We firmly believe that the future of the Church, the coming of the Kingdom, and the judgment of God on the world are tied up with these movements.

CONCILIUM

All back issues are still in print: available from bookshops (price £3.50) or direct from the publisher (£3.50/US$7.45/Can$8.55 including postage and packing).

T. & T. CLARK LIMITED
36 George Street, Edinburgh EH2 2LQ, Scotland

CONCILIUM 1983

NEW RELIGIOUS MOVEMENTS

LITURGY: A CREATIVE TRADITION

MARTYRDOM TODAY

CHURCH AND PEACE

INDIFFERENCE TO RELIGION

THEOLOGY AND COSMOLOGY

THE ECUMENICAL COUNCIL AND THE CHURCH CONSTITUTION

MARY IN THE CHURCHES

JOB AND THE SILENCE OF GOD

TWENTY YEARS OF CONCILIUM— RETROSPECT AND PROSPECT

All back issues are still in print: available from bookshops (price £3.50) or direct from the publisher (£3.85/US$7.45/Can$8.55 including postage and packing).

T. & T. CLARK LTD, 36 GEORGE STREET, EDINBURGH EH2 2LQ, SCOTLAND